# HENLEY AND BURNS.

Bust of Robert Burns, by D. W. Stevenson, R.S.A., in National Wallace Monument.

# HENLEY AND BURNS

Or, THE CRITIC CENSURED,

BEING A COLLECTION OF PAPERS REPLYING TO AN
OFFENSIVE CRITIQUE ON THE LIFE, GENIUS,
AND ACHIEVEMENTS OF

## THE SCOTTISH POET.

COLLECTED AND EDITED BY

## JOHN D. ROSS, LL.D.

KENNIKAT PRESS
Port Washington, N. Y./London

HENLEY AND BURNS

First published in 1901
Reissued in 1970 by Kennikat Press
Library of Congress Catalog Card No: 77-105828
ISBN 0-8046-1032-0

Manufactured by Taylor Publishing Company    Dallas, Texas

𝔇𝔢𝔡𝔦𝔠𝔞𝔱𝔢𝔡

TO

THE LOVERS OF BURNS

EVERYWHERE.

## PREFACE.

NEARLY four years ago I struggled through Mr. Henley's remarkable Essay on Robert Burns, and ever since I have wondered at my simplicity and rashness in so doing. It was a weary, uncongenial task, and aroused within me sentiments of anger and amazement. Indeed, the peculiar sensations produced by the reading of that most unsavoury piece of criticism—*that blot upon literature*—are still very vividly impressed upon my imagination, and will make themselves felt for many years to come. And no wonder; a more contemptible or unsatisfactory piece of writing on the subject of Robert Burns never passed through my hands, nor is it at all probable that I shall ever see its like or anything akin to it again. The reception it has met with at the hands of all honest admirers and critics will no doubt deter any literary mercenary ever attempting to arouse interest in himself by a similar performance, either purely for personal notoriety or "for a fee."

There is one redeeming feature about the Essay—and only one—it was not written by a Scotsman. Thank Heaven for that! No countryman of Burns would be guilty of laying such filth before the world.

So far, I have failed to realize just why Mr. Henley should wish to belittle the "Life, Genius, and Achievements" of Burns in the manner he has done. His tirade of abuse was certainly uncalled for, especially when we consider that the poet has been dead for over a century, and that the whole world to-day pays homage to his genius and greatness. As far as the Essay—if the thing can be called by so dignified a name—is concerned, there is absolutely not a scrap of new information in it. The matter is all second-hand, and, in addition to this, it is placed before the public in so peculiar a form that it is positively unreliable and misleading.

No doubt it is perfectly appropriate when necessary to refer to one or two unpleasant facts in connection with the career of Burns, but Mr. Henley goes far beyond this. He glories in painting the most insignificant old tittle-tattles in the blackest of colours; he presumes, ridicules, insinuates; in fact, he goes so far with his theories, suspicions, and conclusions, that he not only misleads the reader, but insults him as well by publishing, and thereby inviting him to read, such trash. I have no patience with such literary work, no matter how cunning or brilliant the phraseology may be. It is nauseating in the extreme.

The few papers reprinted herewith speak for themselves. Most of them were stowed away in my library, labelled "An Appendix to the Centenary Burns," but on determining to issue them in permanent form I concluded that a more appropriate title was necessary, and so decided on the one under which they now appear. That they may serve in some measure to counteract the offensive work of Mr. Henley is the sincere wish of the writer, as, indeed, it must be of all lovers of Robert Burns.

JOHN D. ROSS.

UNION COURSE,
   WOODHAVEN,
      NEW YORK, *January, 1901*.

## CONTENTS.

| | PAGE |
|---|---|
| HENLEYISM AND THE FIRST EDITION OF BURNS (*Scotsman*), | 1 |
| MR. HENLEY AND HIS BURNS GLOSSARY (*Edinburgh Evening News*), | 5 |
| MR. HENLEY'S ESSAY ON ROBERT BURNS (*Daily Record*), | 9 |
| A CRITIC SCARIFIED (*Kilmarnock Standard*), | 23 |
| MODERN CROSS-GRAINED HERESIES IN HISTORY—MR. W. E. HENLEY (*Saint Andrew*), | 29 |
| ROBERT BURNS (*Greenock Telegraph*), | 37 |
| CONCERNING VOLUME I. OF THE CENTENARY BURNS (*London Daily Chronicle*), | 40 |
| THE MISREPRESENTATIONS OF A CRITIC, BY THE REV. ARTHUR JOHN LOCKHART, MAINE, | 48 |
| THE LATEST ABOUT BURNS (*Chicago Newspaper*), | 53 |
| SPEECH BY MR. F. FAITHFULL BEGG, M.P., TO THE ROSEBERY BURNS CLUB, GLASGOW, 25TH JANUARY, 1898, | 58 |
| MR. R. WALLACE, M.P., ON BURNS'S CRITICS—AN ADDRESS DELIVERED BEFORE THE LEEDS CALEDONIAN SOCIETY, 25TH JANUARY, 1899, | 74 |
| SHERIFF BRAND ON THE SUBJECT, | 81 |
| THE REV. J. H. M'CULLOCH'S PROTEST—FROM AN ADDRESS DELIVERED BEFORE THE LEITH BURNS CLUB, 25TH JANUARY, 1898, | 86 |
| MR. JOHN SINTON ON THE SUBJECT, | 90 |
| CONCERNING THE ESSAY, BY MR. JOHN S. MACNAB, NEW YORK, | 98 |
| "THE PENURIOUS COCKNEY," | 104 |

# HENLEY AND BURNS.

## HENLEYISM AND THE FIRST EDITION OF BURNS.

*From "The Scotsman," 15th February, 1898.*

Lovers of Burns will rejoice to learn from the large price paid this week for a Kilmarnock edition that, despite the criticism of Mr. W. E. Henley in the Centenary Edition, there are as yet no signs that the poet's popularity is on the wane. Mr. Henley is a Superior Person, and he is conscious of his own superiority. In the first issue of a new weekly publication, entitled *The Outlook*, he refers in a lofty and distant way to the small persons who dared, on the last Burns night, to suggest that this Superior Person had not quite realised the standpoint from which Burns ought to be judged, and is judged by those who understand him. Mr. Henley does not attempt to answer such people—" half-read M.P.'s and Sheriffs, and divines and provosts flushed with literary patriotism." His position is that "Burns is and was ever the Poet of the Uncritical;" and for a Critic to stoop to answer the Uncritical is not to be thought of. But he admits that he was affected by the utterances of the "shoal of provosts, and sheriffs, and divines and the like," and turned for comfort in adversities to Carlyle, only to find "that Carlyle, who couldn't drink and therefore hated liquor, is practically the father of All Them that Babble in Burns Clubs." This excellent critic, whose originality is marked even in the use of capital letters, having "dislimned" the living aspect of the "magnificated" Scottish poet—the words are Mr. Henley's own—turns and rends Thomas Carlyle. "Read the Essay on Burns, the Peasant on the Peasant, and you shall find that despite some points of difference he, so long the 'Sage,' is so closely in touch with the Burns Clubbists of to-day—in sentimentalism, partial knowledge of his subject, disdain of natural and inevitable law"—really one begins to ask who is this literary iconoclast who has come out to destroy our Scottish literary idols? Mr. Henley is a critic with a high reputation for cleverness, but we know that Carlyle was unkind enough to call critics the "flesh flies of literature." Mr. Henley is also a poet; and by no means a bad poet; at least so it is said by those who have read his verses. No doubt the consciousness that he possesses the poetic and the critical gift in combination has led this very Superior Person to magnify the weaknesses of Burns and his worshippers. Yet his exercise has only served to illustrate the lines of Pope—

> "Some have at first for wits, then poets passed;
> Turned critics next, and proved plain fools at last."

It is really very kind of Mr. Henley to attempt to shield Burns from the "Elderly Burnsite," of whom presumably Carlyle is the prototype. But it is not necessary. Rightly or wrongly, Scotsmen will cling to "the Burns Superstition," and will be the better for it. At an important book-sale in Edinburgh this week a Kilmarnock first edition, in an apparently perfect state of preservation, fetched the remarkable price of 545 guineas. The highest price ever before given for a copy of this edition —mutilated, however, and in inferior condition —was £120. Such a figure is undoubtedly a "fancy price." The book is very rare, and to the bibliophile rarity is an all-important consideration in estimating value. But the popularity of the poet, the admiration of the Uncritical, as Mr. Henley would put it, has helped to magnify the price of the book, and the critic's depreciation has had no effect on the market. This will be comforting to "the

## 4   HENLEY AND BURNS.

half-read divines and provosts and sheriffs and M.P.'s," and the rest of "the great mob that whenever a year is 'five-and-twenty days begun' assembles all over Scotland, to drink whisky, and eat haggis, and make speeches in the Idol's praise." To do such things may betray lack of discrimination; but after all it is better than reading Henley.

## MR. HENLEY AND HIS BURNS GLOSSARY.

*From the "Edinburgh Evening News,"*
*16th October, 1897.*

Nemesis has overtaken Robert Burns. He has been edited by Mr. Henley. True, Burns's fate might have been even more tragic. He might have been edited by Professor Saintsbury. Still, the fate of Burns is hard enough. He, the great master of his native language, has been rendered comprehensible by a Cockney! Mr. Henley has undertaken to translate Burns into English. He is an authority on glossaries. Has he not compiled a Dictionary of Slang? He does his duty by Burns's words and phrases as elaborately as by Burns's peccadilloes. It is truly a work of portentous erudition. To prevent the faintest possibility of trouble, the poet's text is flanked by innumerable interpretations and notes, just like a students' torchlight procession escorted by mounted police, while a powerful reserve, in the shape of an overwhelming glossary, brings up the rear. When the average Scotsman, who does remember a word or two of his mother tongue, surveys this vast array, he feels as though a road crusher had gone over his soul. Burns, thus interpreted, is a pitiable spectacle. Mr. Henley has been content to leave nothing either to the brains or the imagination of the reader. A few samples may be interesting. Even an Englishman, one would presume, comprehends, or can guess, what "yon" means. Mr. Henley plants "yonder" carefully alongside wherever the word appears. That it occurs on almost every page is nothing to him. "Braes," again, most people understand. Mr. Henley translates it on the margin, and being a born pedant, gives readers their choice. On one page he translates it for them as "heights," on the next as "slopes." Such familiar words as "ane," "wat," "gang," "mair," "canny," "gie," words which even the touring Yankee and the intelligent foreigner comprehend, Mr. Henley translates religiously every time they occur. That "ilk" and "ilka" mean "each" we learn on almost every page, while contractions like "maunna," "dinna," and "winna," are also interpreted whenever they occur. Let it not be imagined that this is done in a mechanical way. Mr. Henley is nothing if not particular. When Burns "pu'd a rose," pray do not imagine Mr. Henley would "pull" it. He "plucks" it, in a marginal note. We confess to a feeling akin to horror when we do on occasion meet mysterious terms like "fause" and "awa'" and "luve" standing alone and unprotected in their native Doric. Mr. Henley must have nodded occasionally, or perhaps the printers' resources in small type got exhausted. But the glossary is a positive triumph. Never a Doric term could slip through its serried columns. It is promptly collared, and made to explain itself. Have we a noun and a verb spelt the same, meaning the same, Mr. Henley must needs enter them separately, give chapter and verse for their identification. All the unhappy victims of the side-notes are here again. One feels infinite compassion for them. "Aff-hand" is explained, not, of course, "off-hand," that would be common, but "at once," though the expression "aff-loof," by a fine discernment, is rendered "off-hand." What a pleasure scholarship is, to be sure! "Aboon:" why, to explain "aboon" we have a rigmarole of words, extracts, and reference figures which looks like the result of an earthquake in the compositor's "galley." Some of Mr. Henley's refinements are marvellous. "Clavers" is defined as: 1, "Gossip;" 2, "Nonsense," each with references after the style of the Shorter Catechism. "Clatter" has no less than five definitions. "Sough" has four. There are interesting facts about Scottish life. "Bannocks" are "soft cakes." A "collie" is: 1, "A general," and sometimes a particular name for country curs (R.B.); 2, "A sheep dog." It is news to learn that the cottar's "lyart haffets" were "discoloured by decay or old age." "Rab" finds a place. "Rab" must needs be explained as the diminutive of Robert. "Rant" means: 1, "To rollick;" 2, "To royster." What in the name of wonder is the difference? And surely, oh surely, a "sumph" is not a "churl." The force of dulness could no further go. It won't do, Mr. Henley. You must do one of two things. Either leave Burns alone, or rewrite him as an appendix to the Dictionary of Slang. As an interpreter you are useless; for the latter alternative you possess the prurient mind and the absence of reverence conducive to entire success.

# MR. HENLEY'S ESSAY ON ROBERT BURNS.

### *From the Glasgow "Daily Record."*

The Essay upon the "Life, Genius, Achievement" of Burns, by Mr. W. E. Henley, opens with the concentration upon the Kirk of Scotland of a light that is almost fierce. The Kirk was an offensive, narrowing, and perverting tyranny, opposed alike to popular liberty and happiness. It was that when 1759 brought Burns, the most popular and anti-clerical poet of his country.

"He came of the people on both sides—he had a high courage, a proud heart, a daring mind, a matchless gift of speech, an abundance of humour and wit and fire. He was a poet in whom were quintessentialised the elements of the Vernacular Genius. . . . . . and in the matter of the Kirk he did for the people a piece of service equal and similar to that which was done on other lines and in other spheres by Hutcheson and Hume and Adam Smith. He was apostle and avenger as well as maker. He did more than give Scotland songs to sing and rhymes to read. He showed that laughter and the joy of life need be no crimes, and that freedom of thought and sentiment and action is within the reach of him that will stretch forth his hand to take it. He pushed his demonstration to extremes. . . . . no doubt, too, he died of his effort—and himself . . . . if he fell in mid-assault he found, despite the circumstances of his passing, the best death man can find. He had faults and failings not a few. But he was ever a leader among men; and if the manner of his leading were not seldom reckless . . . . . it will be found in the long run that he led for truth—the truth which 'maketh free;' so that the Scotland he loved so well, and took such pride in honouring, could scarce have been the Scotland she is, had he not been."

So the point of view changes. Carlyle shows us Burns the sincere man; Taine regards him as the mouth-piece of modern democracy; Henley sees in him the enemy of clerical tyranny. Their views are all right; they are all partial. A larger truth includes them all. The distinction of grouping Mr. Henley with Carlyle and Taine is conferred upon him almost unconsciously, and that statement may be read as evidence of the depth of the impression he makes. The assortment hardly seems of our making. Mr Henley assorts himself with Carlyle and Taine, and in their company, without either qualification or comparison, let him stand.

The introduction is followed by a biographical sketch of Burns, scintillating with pithy things. This is true even when they do not command absolute concurrence. Burns, for example, is called "ever an indifferent Shakespearean," and "the absurd line" is quoted—"Here Douglas forms wild Shakespeare into plan." The line is *ex facie* absurd enough, but is it not possible that the opinion it expresses was the actor's into whose mouth Burns put the words?

## HENLEY AND BURNS.   11

Of women—"apparently he held it an honour to be admired by him." Burns himself gives the arrow its point. After reference to the "Welcome" these passages come. "Burns was first and last a peasant," "absolutely of his station and his time," and if we are to read his baser, lewder, more ribald verses aright, we must read them relatively to the audience to which they were addressed. "As for reading them," says Mr. Henley, "in Victorian terms—that way madness lies: madness, and a Burns that by no process known to gods or men could ever have existed save in the lubber-land of some Pious Editor's dream." In such writing is the "pith o' sense."

The reader has by this early time made the discovery that Mr. Henley is not one of the flock of amiable birds that "in their little nests agree." He is a literary Berserker, and loves battle. A case in point has reference to Burns as farmer, concerning whom it is asked how Mossgiel could have prospered under Rab the Ranter. Mr. Henley accepts the confession concerning the dog returning to his vomit. Misfortune sent Burns to folly. Otherwise, the poet says: "In spite of the Devil, the world, and the flesh, I believe I should have been a wise man." Since Mr. Henley concurs in Burns's confession of a propensity for vomit, why disallow the conditional claim of wisdom? "His head was full of other things than crops and cattle." So Mr. Henley says of Burns, and raises a doubt whether he possessed the qualities that make a husbandman—whether, in short, as a farmer he was not a failure. Let us go on sixty pages to try Mr. Henley by himself. "Ellisland was a mistake." Burns had seen his father fail at Mount Oliphant and Lochlie, he shared Gilbert's failure at Mossgiel—"By no fault of his own, but owing to the circumstance that he had taken a holding out of which he could not make his rent, he failed himself at Ellisland." In this case, it matters little whether he was scarce or wholly "cut out for a successful farmer." Genius, temperament, consciousness of capacity, are irrelevant subjects of discussion. It matters nothing, in this connection, whether or not life meant to Burns "largely, if not wholly, Wine and Women and Song." The point is that all the farms he was ever connected with were commercial mistakes to their tenants. The farms, not the farmers, were failures. They were poor in quality, high in rent, and in falling short of commercial success, Burns, the poet-farmer, only shared the fate of many good farmers who were not poets. That his head was too full of other things is a speculation which has no bearing upon land values.

A small error may be corrected in passing. Mr. Henley mentions in a note that Burns told Ramsay of Auchtertyre that he owed his

Jacobitism to the plundering and unhousing (1715) of his grandfather, who was gardener to Earl Marischal at Inveraray. The reference is to Ramsay of Ochtertyre, who makes allusion to Inverury. The passage is erroneous, Burns's grandfather was Robert Burnes, who, in 1715, held the farm of Kinmonth, and, in 1721, removed to Clochnahill, both in Mearns. The story of plundering and unhousing is purely mythical.

Leaving the farm, Mr. Henley next starts Burns "on his career as amorist at large," and then turns to his poetry, for "at last the hour of the Vernacular Muse has come." These subjects may be taken as here stated.

Let it be said at the outset that Mr. Henley is a marvel, for he can keep his head when talking of the loves of Burns. He has contempt only for the fanatics who have coined a "tame, proper Burns" and offered him as a substitute "for the lewd, amazing peasant of genius, the inspired faun" whom Mr. Henley knows. He finds in Burns a passionate regard for women, without chivalry, a strong sense of fatherhood and tender concern for wife and weans, combined with an unchecked "resolve for pleasure." Still, "Burns was first and last enamoured of the woman he made his wife." Anne Park, however, was his mistress during marriage, the last "who has a name." Currie mentions another, innominate — "accidental complaint," &c. Thereat the inspired faun is left wallowing.

Let us, by all means, put sentiment aside as an encumbrance, but it is impossible to accept Mr. Henley's logic. He speaks of a knowledge of Burns, as if that could be an influence upon reason which is itself in doubt. His want of knowledge of Burns may be his disqualification as judge. He miscalculates his own language so far as to leave an impression that he confounds virility with nastiness, and cleanly morals with milk-and-watery sentimentalism. Regarding Burns in Dumfries, what is wanted is proof. He was not a model, but if he were black as a mulatto that is no reason for making him a nigger outright. Mr. Henley has lent far too lenient an ear to the chirpings of the gutter-birds of Dumfries. He convicts Burns of the blackest conduct upon evidence which, if imported into another case, would not convict a dog of stealing a bone.

Mr. Henley treats Highland Mary in similar fashion. He adduces Burns himself as witness "that they met and parted under extremely suspicious circumstances." With all deference, Burns says nothing which can fairly bear such a construction. Let us turn back. The note to "My Highland Lassie, O!" is—as the annotator says of the story of Highland Mary—"a very pretty tangle." It is said that "The 'Highland Lassie' was Mary

Campbell." We are not sure of it. There is no evidence of it, and the dogmatic statement of it as an unquestionable fact is unsupported by a tittle of proof. Nay, more, when Mr. Henley came to write his essay, their identity became to him only a "strong probability." Between the writing of the Note and that of the Essay he subsided from cock-sureness into a more dubious and far more judicial state of mind.

Next comes, in the Notes, a callous suggestion of the identity of Mary with "a certain Mary Campbell of indifferent repute," *i.e.*, poor Mary of Dundonald. Further on it is said somewhat coarsely: "Mary Campbell has come to be regarded less as an average Scots peasant to whom a merry-begot was then, if not a necessary of life, at all events the commonest effect of luck, than as a sort of bare-legged Beatrice — a Spiritualised Ideal of Peasant womanhood." Surely there is in this as little chivalry as in Burns's conduct to Maria Riddell and Mrs. Oswald of Auchencruive. It betrays no sign of respect for a woman whether Ideal or Real, whether Mary Campbell or another, whom Burns has immortalised. Her cult is an absurdity, a craze! "The Mary Campbell of tradition is a figment of the General Brain." Reference is also made to the "underhandedness of the engagement" between Burns and his

Highland Lassie, but is this serious? Does anyone confide to the world his amorous peccadilloes? Does the world stop to listen? Had Burns no right to reticence? Mr. Henley, further, argues that unless Mary was a paragon, the bronze at Dunoon is a witness to a national delusion. But suppose the nation had nothing to do with the bronze, what becomes of the delusion? Because a handful of Mariolatrous fanatics choose to make grimaces in the face of the moon, is Scotland's reason to be impugned? Better for Mr. Henley to lose his head anywhere than here. Keeping a single eye to the songs she inspired, the personal identity of the woman, is, in reality, a matter of slight consequence. What if she be a figment, not only of the general brain, but of Burns's imagination? Shall we for that reason place the less value upon the pathetic music with which she filled his heart? Suppose Mary the creation of Burns, let us not do him the dishonour of flinging mud at his ideal. Suppose her a reality, and why should we blacken gratuitously a memory enshrined in some of his sweetest verse? Burns has made "Mary in Heaven" more real than any creature of flesh and blood, any Mary on earth. Having a profound respect for Burns, we approach with co-ordinate respect the source from which, in this matter, he drew inspiration. Mr. Henley has marred his Essay with purely excrescent contentiousness and cynicism.

Again, in reference to Burns in Dumfries, Mr. Henley states opinions which are not borne out by facts. Of that entire period he says "the story is a story of decadence." All the world knows what it means to shrug the shoulders and say of a man—"gone down." Virtually, that is Mr. Henley's comment on Burns. Look at Burns's beginnings, his youth's battle, the raging conflict of his manhood, and then say if it is not ludicrous to speak of his being so far a failure "that he had nothing to look forward to but promotion in the Excise." All he asked was a collectorship *plus* the literary leisure it would have secured him. Nine out of ten would call a similar look-out a brilliant proof of success in life; and, had he lived, his modest hope had almost surely been gratified. Mr. Henley, however, persists in the whisky-*cum*-prostitute theory of physical decline, to which the assumption of intellectual decline must somehow be fitted.

The essayist echoes the annotator. The latter says, "The best of time had passed for Burns ere his connection with Thomson began," "His way of life was falling into the sere and yellow leaf," "His inspiration was its old rapturous irresistible self no longer." The position taken up in these clauses has been so often proved untenable that they almost amount to perversion of plain facts. Burns's first letter to Thomson is dated 16th September,

1792, and the songs written by him after that date include "The Lea Rig," "Highland Mary," "Duncan Gray," "Here's a health to them that's awa'," "Poortith cauld and restless love," "Lord Gregory," "Whistle, an' I'll come to you, my lad," "Scots wha ha'e," "Thou hast left me ever, Jamie," "A red, red rose," "Ca' the yowes to the knowes," "My Nannie's awa'," "A man's a man for a' that," and "O wert thou in the cauld blast." Burns, in short, wrote some of his favourite songs after the date when the best of time for him had passed and his inspiration was drying up!

The annotation, moreover, affects to draw a distinction between the Thomson and the Johnson songs. The former, we are told, although exceptions are admitted, "have not the fresh sweetness and the unflagging spirit of his *Museum* numbers." If there be anything in the distinction, how does it happen that Burns wrote "Whistle an' I'll come to you," with its borrowed chorus, in the same year that he wrote "Scots wha ha'e" and "Thou hast left me ever, Jamie"? How does it happen that "A red, red rose," in which (*vide* first paper) there is not an original thought, was sent, not to Thomson, but to Johnson, in the same way that "My Nannie's awa'" was written for Thomson? The fact is that Burns was writing simultaneously for both publications, and that he was tinkering, improving, and adding to old

## HENLEY AND BURNS. 19

songs for both Thomson and Johnson at the same time that he was composing some of his best and most perfectly original lyrics. Literary decadence at Dumfries, in short, will not hold. It is accordingly impossible to agree with Mr. Henley that Burns "left the world at the right moment for himself and for his fame." A careful study of Burns's letters and poetry leads to the opposite opinion that he was rising, not sinking, when he died. He was rising into a serener air, above the passions and grosser appetites which shook his life.

Mr. Henley returns to the charge that Burns was the "satirist and singer of a parish," "the last of a school," and that his "adaptation of old rhymes and folk-songs to modern uses constitutes his chief claim to perennial acceptance." But we take exception to the statement in the first volume that Burns was "not the founder of a dynasty, but the heir to a flourishing tradition, and the last of an ancient line." In our judgment, he opened a new era in both Scottish song and Scottish thought. He certainly borrowed a few rough and broken bricks from the past, but he built for the future. He made the vernacular an instrument for phrasing a new Gospel. He did not fight the Kirk, raise his people, and help to make Scotland what she is by either perpetuating an old stave, or building upon a foundation laid by the old makkars. He did all these things by making the old form the vehicle of a new message, and he lives in the latter and not in its form. The genius of the architect makes stone and lime poetical. He puts fire into matter—Burns looked so far into modern times that he saw past them, and reached a point which, in respect of inseeing, penetrating wisdom, still lies ahead of the mass of his countrymen. It is, surely, most illogical to give him to the past, because he took from it sundry scraps of verse and, we are told, adapted them to modern uses. That assuredly looks less like closing an old than opening a new line. It is, nevertheless, contended that, by reason of his indebtedness, Burns substantiated his right to be called a national poet. At the same time he was parochial—"a fact which only the Common Burnsite could be crazy enough or pig-headed enough to deny." Finally, we are told that he was the most broadly or genuinely human of the lyrists of his race. So that, at one and the same time, he is parochial, national, and broadly human! There is no ambiguity here, and if it were desirable to belabour Mr. Henley with the weapons he uses in his encounters with his nameless antagonist, the following case might be elaborated: The "Common Burnsite" reappears as "sentimental, ignorant, uncritical," and if these adjectives *plus* " crazy " and " pig-headed," previously quoted, describe him, there cannot be a great difference between him and the Uncommon

Burnsite who trips himself up in tilting at windmills.

Not in such terms is it proposed to take leave of Mr. Henley. When, however, he resorts to forensic debate, he doffs the ermine. In the Notes there are evidences that he has allowed his critics to unsettle his judgment, and the consequence is felt in the Essay. He cannot run off into a succession of sidings without impairing the unity of his plan. The Essay lacks cohesion, and that finished adjustment of parts to a complete design which corresponds with symmetry and proportion in architecture. Mr. Henley has a weakness for the assertion of his differences from other people. It diverts his attention not only from the balance of parts in an intellectual structure rising evenly from a foundation stone to a finial that is inevitable, but from Burns the Thinker.

Burns was more than anti-clerical. He was a positive religious and ethical force. He was, and is, a political influence. Carry his social views into practice—as they will be some day—and society will be reformed, remodelled. These are points upon which Mr. Henley might well have written, " and let puir damned bodies be " who venture to differ from him on the minor issues of a great career. Mr. Henley is large enough, generous, and full-blooded enough to appreciate and be just to Burns. Witness what he says of the world of Burns living for us in his pictures—"And many such attempts at reconstruction as 'The Earthly Paradise' and 'The Idylls of the King' will fade far away, dissolve, and be quite forgotten ere these pictures disfeature or dislimn, . . . . and, in the sequel, he is found to have a place of his own in the first flight of English poets after Milton, Chaucer, Shakespeare." We would not ask at Mr. Henley's hands more of such praise, but more of the thought that led to and inspired it, more of the thought that it suggests and that must have followed it.

## A CRITIC SCARIFIED.

*From the "Kilmarnock Standard," 21st January, 1899.*

Our southern neighbours have sarcastically dubbed the twenty-fifth the festival of St. Robert, but the truth is that this particular date in January has come to be regarded as one of the set times of the nation for social intercourse, apart altogether from what at first it was undoubtedly meant to commemorate. The Scot, outwith the bounds of his native country, is proverbially clannish, and eagerly embraces every opportunity calculated to bring together his fellow-countrymen in sufficient numbers to realise to the full the heart-stirring sentiments embalmed in "Auld Langsyne," which might very appropriately be adopted as the National Anthem. Thoughts of home and fatherland cannot of course account for the outburst of enthusiasm in every nook and corner of Scotland at the end of each recurring January—a phenomenon which, in spite of the ridicule and sneering of foreigners, has preserved its spontaneity and fervour undiminished for more than a hundred years. Why is this so? Had it been mere hero-worship, enthusiasm would inevitably have waned, as the hero receded down the vista of time. It is because the national poet of Scotland is the exponent of the national sentiment and aspirations in a degree never attained by any other poet, ancient or modern, that he has gained such a hold upon the people—a hold so deep and powerful that Burns and Scotland are with them almost interchangeable terms. He is, *par excellence*, "the patriot and the patriot bard," uttering in words of fire, easily understood of the people, the deep feelings of the heart which found no adequate expression till he took them in hand for melodious interpretation. Other nations have their national poets who occupy high seats in the Temple of Fame, but none of them, not even excepting Shakespeare, has so captivated the common people that his lines have become as proverbs amongst them. The vernacular in which Burns wrote his most inspired verses is to Cockney critics almost an unknown tongue, and hence it is that writers like Mr. Henley, in estimating the achievements of Burns, do so in a twilight illumined only by whatever amount of light they happen to carry in their hands. In his recent Essay in the Centenary Burns, which has caused so much stir, Mr. Henley gropes about with a very poor rushlight indeed, which, while revealing to him the puddles on the road and the gaps in the fences, leaves all else in darkness. He evidently approached his subject with strong prejudices and preconceived notions, the products of surprising ignorance, not only of the Scotland of Burns's time, but even of the Scotland of to-day. In fact, his superficial summing up of the environment of Burns partakes more of the nature of a national libel than an attack on the personality of the Bard. Some of his assertions are simply astounding, such as that Burns was the product of a tyrannical, narrowing, and perverting Kirk, allied with the Parish School, which was established "to provide its creatures with such teaching as it seemed desirable," whereas the truth is that the Poet's father was a theological rebel, only less pronounced than his illustrious son, and Robert Burns, to all intents and purposes, was educated at home. On the same level of crass ignorance of our social history must be placed the elegant compliment that the Scotland Burns represents "is the Scotland out of which the wild Whigs crushed the taste for everything but fornication." At the time of its publication, the Essay was exposed to the scathing criticism of nearly every representative man of letters who claimed kindred north of the Tweed, but the Burns cult preserved a remarkable silence, strongly suggestive either of contempt for the whole performance, or a tacit understanding to give it as little gratuitous advertisement as possible.

In the 1899 issue of the "Burns Chronicle," the editor, Mr. M'Naught, gives prominence to a vigorous and trenchant article in which Mr. Henley is severely handled, and to most excellent purpose. It is from the pen of Mr. Wm. M'Ilwraith, a Scot resident in Wolverhampton, who has already earned more than a local reputation by his literary publications, more especially those dealing with the modern craze known as Theosophy. At the outset he accuses Henley of borrowing from Robert Louis Stevenson and Carlyle as much as suited his purpose, and then turning round and abusing both because their ultimate conclusions differ from his own. "The Cottar's Saturday Night" is adduced as an illustration of his ignorance of the Scottish peasantry whom he writes down with so much gusto and cocksureness. Of this piece, Mr. Henley says "it was doomed to popularity from the first, being of its essence sentimental, and therefore untrue." Every Scotsman whose memory carries him no further back than two decades, can give the lie to this assertion, and Mr. M'Ilwraith does not scruple to do so in the plainest of terms, drawing upon his recollections of forty years ago, when it was very exceptional to find a rural cottage in which family worship was not regularly observed. In collecting his materials for the formation of his estimate of Burns, Mr. Henley rejected "The Cottar's Saturday Night," and all compositions of a like nature. They neither suited his purpose nor coincided with his personal tastes. He preferred the "Libel Summons," the "Epistle to a Tailor," and the ribald effusions of the "Merry Muses" which were foisted on the name of Burns a quarter of a century after he had gone to his account. For this peculiar *penchant* in the way of poetic literature, Mr. M'Ilwraith takes him soundly to task by asking him if the social history of any country is to be found only in skulduddery records and annals of Criminal Courts? When the English people are prepared to accept the representations of the Elizabethan dramatists and the novels of Fielding as the mirror of England in the past it will be time enough to point to the mote in the eye of Scotland. The filth and obscenity of the "Merry Muses" Mr. Henley considers "unique and precious, inasmuch as they bear witness to an admirable talent," and he speaks of the volume as if Burns were either its author or editor, though he nowhere says straight out that either charge can be brought home to him. The whole subject was exhaustively dealt with by Mr. M'Naught in the third number of the "Chronicle," but Mr. Henley ignores this, as all else that is against him, preferring to deal by inuendo when direct assault would be his undoing. On this head Mr. M'Ilwraith dismisses him with the remark that "all men have a bias from which it is difficult to set themselves free, and we need not marvel if Mr. Henley has a bias to bathing in polluted waters while his nature revolts against the waters of the limpid stream." This bias runs through and vitiates and vulgarises the whole Essay. Where Burns or his contemporaries cannot be condemned by direct evidence, all manner of gossip and apocryphal testimony are lugged in to give piquancy to the narrative, though again and again he is compelled to acknowledge that the damaging stories he recounts so unctuously are "utterly unauthenticated." Even Saunders Tait, the Tarbolton rhymer, is dragged in to demonstrate that the Burns family swindled their landlord when tenants in Lochlea, in ludicrous unconsciousness that any such charge reflects more upon honest William Burns than any individual member of his family. Mr. M'Ilwraith also disposes successfully of the "plagiarism" ascribed to Burns, and he writes warmly and convincingly of the unworthy misconstructions contained in the Essay concerning Highland Mary and Clarinda. His criticism of Mr. Henley's effort is undoubtedly the best which has yet appeared, and we have no doubt it will be eagerly read and appreciated by every patriotic Scotsman both at home and abroad.

# MODERN CROSS-GRAINED HERESIES IN HISTORY.

## Mr. W. E. Henley.

### From "Saint Andrew," 17th March, 1899.

Nothing surprises so much as the barefaced coolness with which manufacturers of literature for Southern readers promulgate heresies for Scottish History. The ingenuity of their themes and theories as much displays the ill-digested information of the makers as the credulous receptivity of their customers in England. Among moderns, twisted criticism of plain Scottish facts and principles in the rule of Church and State had its most brilliant exponent in Henry Thomas Buckle, who, in the "History of Civilisation in England," delights in picturing the Scots as a kind of superior "Yahoos," not deficient in some qualities which bloom in the nineteenth century in Southern latitudes. A sincere disciple and flattering imitator of Buckle is Mr. W. E. Henley, the smart compiler of an Essay on Burns, for which the poet's countrymen ought to be thankful as affording an amusing satire upon some of the great forces which have made Scotland no mean, inglorious kingdom. Mr. Henley salutes his subject by an affront to the Kirk of Scotland of 1759, which he pillories as a tyranny " potent enough to make life miserable, to warp the characters of men and women, and to turn the tempers and affections of many from the kindly, natural way." Then, with designed endeavour after Shakespearean smartness, Mr. Henley clinches his assertion by what seems to be a perilous paraphrase of Buckle's account of Hutcheson's doctrines (Buckle: vol. iii. p. 295; edit. 1891); and thereafter sets himself to prove what is not true, that Burns was an antagonist of the Kirk —" a peasant in revolt against the Kirk." Since his Essay appeared, Mr. Henley has been hard on " half-read divines, and provosts, and sheriffs, and M.P.'s " who, after all, know a little about their country and their poet. But all Buckle's reading, and he had pleasure in exploring many dirty conduits, left him ignorant of Scottish History and the Scottish spirit. To Buckle, be it said, the Kirk was only a *bête noire* sometimes; to Mr. Henley it is always. A more brilliant writer than either, and an English Dissenter to boot, Defoe, as an eyewitness of the influence of the Church, had a different opinion. "Another thing I cannot omit, in which the Constitution of the Church of Scotland is singular and differing from her neighbours, and this is, that not the least room is left here for the popular charge of priestcraft, etc., . . . . and I must acknowledge that there seems to be such an appearance of the Spirit and presence of God with and in this Church as is not at this time to be seen in any Church in the world." Why did the much-read Buckle not cite Defoe? Mr. Henley also conjures with Adam Smith's name. What did Smith say of this affronted Church: "The most opulent Church in Christendom does not maintain better the uniformity of faith, the fervour of devotion, the spirit of order, regularity, and austere morals in the great body of the people than this very poorly endowed Church of Scotland." Burns was then the ploughboy of Mount Oliphant. This faith, order, morality, were maintained by a clergy whose annual stipend was £73 on the average—a very cheap police! Why did Buckle not quote Smith?

Mr. Henley practically accuses the Kirk of obliterating the vernacular school of writers— a most absurd proposition, of which more anon (*pace* Mr. T. F. Henderson). Mr. Henley's hood is puffed to its largest when he insinuates that the Covenanted Church of the Reformers, the "wild Whigs" of his imagination, was the cause of the immorality of Burns's day (note, p. 265). He reiterates the same impertinent diatribe (p. 252) when he refers to "the poor-living, lewd, grimy, free-spoken, ribald, old

Scots peasant-world." In a foot-note he speaks of some bucolic virtues. These unpardonable slanders on the Scotch in "general," and the Scottish peasants in particular, enable Mr. Henley to display a very offensive vulgarity and parsimony of the truth when he says (p. 236), "The Scots peasant . . . . fed so cheaply that even on high days and holidays his diet (as set forth in 'The Blithesome Bridal') consisted largely in preparations of meal and vegetables and what is technically known as 'offal.'" The author is happily addressing ignorant Southerns, not even "half-read" Scots. However, it need not be imagined that Mr. Henley can translate the Scots language of the poem he refers to, else he would not assert that the viands specified in it are such common fare, consisting as they did of six different soups, eight varieties of fish, including shell-fish, six varieties of flesh (roasts, salted meat, nolt feet, haggis, tripe, sheep's head), three kinds of bread (oaten, barley, and wheaten), cheese, new ale, and brandy. We hope the critic has such variegated fare every day!

But it is mean slander to brand the Scots peasantry as lewd, grimy, ribald livers. After investigation we challenge Mr. Henley *et hoc genus omne* to disprove the fact here stated that the record of crime, immorality, loose living, in every parish wherein Burns resided shows less by one-half—by fifty to seventy per cent.—in that epoch, than it does in the same parishes to-day, and this latter after a century's more unclerical civilisation, together with the newer journalism, and Burns as well as Mr. Henley thrown in as antidotes to the alleged tyranny of the Kirk. Moreover, there is proof sufficient to support the retort that the peasantry generally were far from being lewd, grimy, and ribald, a few coarse songs and ballads notwithstanding. But why did Mr. Henley illustrate Burns's day by this poem published half a century before the poet was born.? Burns's father was not a lewd, ribald peasant. Nor was Burns's ideal Cottar. Might not, then, Mr. Henley have pictured out of Scots Song a likelier rustic, say "The Happy Clown:"—

> "Now by a silver stream he lies
> And angles with his baits and flies,"

who

> "for attending well his bees
> Enjoys their sweet reward."

Did not Sir John Clerk picture a contemporary happy miller and his thrifty wife:

> "For meal and malt she does na' want,
> Nor anything that's dainty,
> And now and then a keckling hen
> To lay her eggs in plenty."

Is Mr. Henley under the delusion that Scotland was always cursed with famine, or plagued with English interference, so that the peasantry possessed no bestial nor poultry, far less salmon and river trout to feed on—but only "offal"? What a Scots song says of the shepherd is as true of the lowland cottar:

> "He lives content, and envies none;
> Not even a monarch on his throne
> Though he the royal sceptre sways,
> Has such pleasant holidays."

The ruins of countless cots with their steadings and gardens throughout the country are a visible reminder of the comforts of the whilom lower orders. The "Heather Jock" of a late song was, in Burns's day, a real character, who

> "Blass'd the burns and speared the fish
> Jock had mony a dainty dish;—
> The best o' moorfowl and black cock,
> Aye graced the board of Heather Jock."

The possible annual product of the salmon rivers in Scotland in 1709 was 40,000 barrels for export, so that fish was abundant in the eighteenth century. The peasantry were also wont to lay in stock of preserved fish, "marts," and bacon for their winter consumpt, so that, as far as our information goes, the ordinary married ploughman might truthfully sing Burns's own adapted lyric: "There's nae life like the ploughman's in the merry month of May."

Mr. Henley as wrongly again declares that the peasant "was a creature of the Kirk," and provided " with such teaching as it deemed desirable." This is pure moonshine shed from Buckle. From 1696 onward the appointment of parish teachers was vested in the whole of the heritors, among whom the parish minister was reckoned as one, and consequently it would be less ridiculous to declare that the Medical Faculty was a creature of the Church, as well as their patients, because, formerly, Parochial Boards, on which parish ministers *ex officio* sat, appointed doctors for the paupers. Mr. Henley is fatally out of accord with the facts and spirit of Scottish History. A writer who boldly affects the libeller running amuck, who imagines in 1896 that the poems of Alexander Tait were a "discovery" although they are copiously quoted in " The Contemporaries of Burns " nearly 60 years ago, who on no just ground whatever accuses the wide-awake Dr. Auld (the minister whom Burns personally revered) of an illegal act regarding Burns's marriage simply because Mr. Henley is not conversant with Northern ecclesiastical law, nor yet with the late Dr. Edgar's explanation of Auld's Church procedure, is well fitted to produce cross-grained heresies in Scottish History.

To Mr. Henley's credit be it said, however, he rightly concludes that, " The best of many nameless singers live in Burns's songs . . . nor could his songs have been so far wandered as they are, nor so long lived as they must be, had these innominates not lived their lyric life before him" (p. 323). It would have satisfied a "half-read" critic to have seen it stated that long before "there was secreted the certainty of a revulsion" against the ascendency of the Kirk in Mr. Henley, this idea was promulgated in similar terms by a greater man—Goethe.

HISTORICUS.

## ROBERT BURNS.

*From "The Greenock Telegraph," 24th January, 1898.*

The onward march of this peasant-born son of genius is simply marvellous. His lustre is not dimmed but brightened by the hand of time. We are told by some of his critics, who desire to belittle his claim to original genius, that he was an adapter, and to some extent, especially in his songs, a plagiarist. We are also told by others, such as Mr. W. E. Henley, that he was a bad man, a stupidly-proud egotist, a buck, a bacchanalian, and much more that ought to depreciate his value as a popular idol. We are further informed by some illustrious authorities that his serious poems are only fit to be forgotten, by others that his songs are silly, and by still others that his whole works are too tedious to engage human attention. An extract from Aubrey de Vere's recollections of Lord Tennyson, in which he narrates a most suggestive conversation he had with the author of "In Memoriam" relative to the Ayrshire Wonder is most interesting.

"'Read the exquisite songs of Burns,' he [Tennyson] exclaimed. 'In shape each of them has the perfection of the berry; in light the radiance of the dew-drop; you forget for its sake those stupid things, his serious pieces!' The same day I met Wordsworth, and named Burns to him. Wordsworth praised him even more vehemently than Tennyson had done, as the great genius who had brought Poetry back to Nature; but ended: 'Of course I refer to his serious efforts, such as the *Cottar's Saturday Night*; those foolish little amatory songs of his one has to forget.' I told the tale to Henry Taylor that evening, and his answer was: 'Burns's exquisite songs and Burns's serious efforts are to me alike tedious and disagreeable reading.' So much for the infallibility of poets in their own art!"

When three such men differ so widely about Robert Burns, why should the average thinking man take his "gospel" from W. E. Henley or any other popularity-seeking and shilling-hunting biographer? Most Scotsmen can read and reflect, and they do not require a Southron, however able, to dish up Burns for them. They know all about the poet's high-strung passions, his woeful failings, and the tragic last ten years of his brief self-consuming career. But they do not see any good that can come from poking up ancient dust-heaps, as Mr. Henley has done. It must be admitted that "Burns's Life, Genius, and Achievement" is a brilliant and searching literary performance, but what about its hardly-concealed purpose, its ungenerous insinuations, its grudging admissions, and its narrow, earthy

## HENLEY AND BURNS.

tone? The design of W. E. Henley is to belittle Burns, not as a poet—that is beyond his power—but as a man. Our shilling critic puts the inspired peasant on a dissecting table and goes over him bone by bone, rib by rib, exposing all his faults, and revelling in his shortcomings. The work, if correct in a literary sense and couched in eloquent phraseology, is somewhat ghoulish in style and aim, and in that way is not the most perfect art. Why should Carlyle's inner life have been held up to the world by Froude, and Burns by Henley? Is it because they were divinely-gifted Scotsmen? Why should the sacrificers always hail from the South? Is the exposure of human foibles a work peculiarly gratifying to some English natures? If so, why should they wander from home? What about that muck-heap of immorality, written by one William Shakespeare, called "Pericles, Prince of Tyre?" What about the immoralities of Ben Johnson, Beaumont, and Fletcher, Congreve, Pope? Burns wrote "fleshly" stuff, but he never condescended to the calculated wantonness of "May and December," or "The Wife of Bath." If we are going to have exposure, let us have it all round.

## CONCERNING VOLUME I. OF THE CENTENARY BURNS.

### From "The London Daily Chronicle," 21st April, 1896.

Let us get our grumble over and have done with it: after a fair trial, we must condemn the binding of this book as neither beautiful nor convenient. The grey pasteboard sides and flat linen back, with a label picked out in red, are certainly unusual, and at first sight quaint enough. But the touch of the book is not agreeable; it suggests a bundle of papers rather loosely filed, and when the boards begin to buckle, as they presently do, the volume will neither shut close nor lie open. No—the binding is curiously infelicitous. Why should a standard edition affect an air of oddity? A standard edition it certainly promises to be—"a king every inch of it" among many competitors, "but without the trappings of a king."

We say "promises to be," for though the performance in this volume is altogether excellent, it represents, after all, but a quarter of the editors' task, and the most "kittle" part is yet to come. Their prospectus sets forth, as follows, the principle of arrangement which they have adopted:—

"It is not forgotten that much has been foisted upon Burns which he did not write: nor that much which he wrote but did not approve—much, at all events, from which he withheld the sanction of print—has been included in his published achievement in the course of years. And with a view to sundering, in so far as may be, the chaff from the grain, the editors have deemed it advisable to distinguish between the pieces on which Burns set and those on which he did not set his *imprimatur*. They have decided, that is, to rearrange the former according to their several dates of publication in the author's own editions, and to deal with the others, each after its kind, upon a definite principle of classification; they will begin, in fact, with the contents of the Kilmarnock and the Edinburgh issues, and they will pass therefrom to the Posthumous Pieces, the Songs, and the Unauthenticated Verses."

In this volume, then, we have the poems published at Kilmarnock in 1786, and the additional poems which appeared in the Edinburgh issues of 1787 and 1793. With respect to these, no question of authenticity arises, and the sifting and winnowing, which will be necessary later on, do not come into play. Yet even in this volume the editors' task, as they have conceived and executed it, has been sufficiently laborious. They have collated not only all the editions published during the poet's lifetime, but all available manuscripts—and of Burns's MSS. there is no end. In almost all of these there are various readings, or at least various spellings; and many of the orthographic variations are of considerable interest, philological or phonetic. As each of the Edinburgh editions occurs in two states, there are practically five printed copies to be collated, and this has been done exhaustively, for the first time. "To indicate every minute variation," says the Bibliographical Note, "would be impossible; but it has been deemed advisable— out of respect both to the reader and to Burns —to set down all the more important." The reader, for his part, may now and then feel that the respect paid him is a little too punctilious. For instance, when Burns, by a common slip of the pen, writes "their" or "there" instead of "they're," the matter is scarcely worth recording. The error is one which occurs every day in hasty writing; it is the merest oversight, of no philological import, nor indicating any peculiarity of pronunciation. Quite different is the case when an English spelling is substituted for a Scotch—for example, *enough* for *eneugh*—or *vice versa*. It is very rarely, however, that the editors can be accused of pettifogging minuteness; and the opposite error, that of overlooking important variants, can never be laid to their charge. In the body of the book—the notes being reserved for the close—they have sought "to redact the best text possible from among the five," and have,

to our thinking, been very well inspired. Their
marginal glossary (not an original device), is
careful and helpful—helpful, we suspect, not
only to the Southron, but to many a degenerate
Scot as well. The notes to each poem open
with a succinct account of the source of its
inspiration, the circumstances of its composi-
tion (so far as they can be ascertained), and the
persons addressed or prominently mentioned in
it. These little historico-biographical disquisi-
tions represent much patient labour, and are
models of compression and order. Most
valuable and interesting, too, are the essays
upon the origin of the principal stanzas used
by Burns, especially that six-line stave which
he "put to all manner of uses and informed
with all manner of sentiments," in such
masterly fashion as to make it peculiarly his
own. It can be traced back to the troubadours
of the eleventh century, was well known in
England in the popular verse of the middle
ages, and had been employed by many Scotch
poets, from "Sir David Lindsay, of the Mount,
Lord Lyon King at Arms," down to Burns's
immediate predecessor and model, the hapless
Robert Fergusson. These researches serve to
emphasise the theory of the editors—

"That Burns, for all his exhibition of some modern ten-
dencies, was not the founder of a dynasty, but the heir to a
flourishing tradition, and the last of an ancient line: that
he is demonstrably the outcome of an environment, and not

in any but the narrowest sense the unnatural birth of Poesy and Time, which he is sometimes held to be."

Talking of the origin of measures, by the way, the plagiarism-hunters have doubtless noticed long ago that Tennyson found the wimpling rhythm of "The Brook" ready made, and applied to the same purpose, in Burns's "Hallowe'en" (stanza xxv.) :—

> "Whyles owre a linn the burnie plays,
>   As thro' the glen it wimpl't;
> Whyles round a rocky scaur it strays,
>   Whyles in a wiel it dimpl't;
> Whyles glitter'd to the nightly rays,
>   Wi' bickerin, dancin' dazzle;
> Whyles cookit underneath the braes,
>   Below the spreading hazel."

We shall have to wait till the last volume appears for Mr. Henley's Essay on the Life and Genius of Burns. We wait with all the livelier hope because Mr. Henley is not (as Mr. Le Galliene said in his haste the other day) a Scotchman. As an Englishman who knows Scotland, who has made a special study of his theme, and to whom it is distinctly congenial, he is exceptionally well situated for forming a sane, sound estimate of the man and the artist. At the same time he seems to take up a rather too haughty position in the opening words of his brief preface to this volume :—

"Burns's verse falls naturally into two main divisions. One, and that the larger, appeals with persistency and force, on the strength of some broadly human qualities, to the world in general: for the reason that the world in general is rich in sentiment but lacks the literary sense. The other, being a notable and lasting contribution to literature, is the concern of comparatively few."

Surely this dichotomy is much too sweeping. Surely the two divisions, which Mr. Henley seems to think as distinct as Middlesex from Surrey, in reality overlap like the circles in the first proposition of Euclid. There are, no doubt, portions of Burns's work which appeal to the sentimentalist alone, and other portions which the artist alone appreciates; but not many poets, we believe, can show so much work that commands in equal measure the admiration of both classes of readers. For Burns was, not only at his best, but in what we may call his average moments, an amazing master of language. It was only when he fell quite below himself—that he failed to give his work that vitality of style which is the essence of literature. It is true that a large part of his poetry is appreciated for different reasons by the general reader and by the man of letters, or at least for reasons which they would formulate differently. But if Mr. Henley means (and we can find no other meaning in his words) that the portions of his work which appeal to the many and those which appeal to the few are entirely separate and mutually exclusive, then we venture to dissent. Whatever else he may have been, Burns was undoubtedly a "Lavengro," a language-lord. We do not know that his diction has ever been analytically studied as it ought to be. It might perhaps be found that his great advantage lay in his mastery, not of one language, but of two imperceptibly shading into each other. True, he was seldom at his best when he confined himself to literary English, but it nevertheless indefinitely widened the range of effects possible to him. There were two keyboards to his instrument. We are not aware that any other poet of equal note ever worked under similar linguistic conditions. There have been poets who wrote only in dialect, and poets who, working for the most part in a literary language, would now and then write a dialect lyric or two. But we know of no two dialects, or language and dialect, that melt into each other so easily, and with so little incongruity, as English and Lowland Scotch. In other cases the line of demarcation is much more hard and fast, and the poet, even where he is master of two idioms, has always to choose between them, so far as any given poem is concerned. But Burns could shift from one language to the other without altering his grammatical framework, or rather from one vocabulary to the other without altering his idiom. He did not lay down one instrument to take up another, but his instrument, as we said before, had a double keyboard. We can scarcely look to Mr. Henley for the close linguistic analysis that would be necessary in order to establish this theory; but we suggest it for his consideration.

# THE MISREPRESENTATIONS OF A CRITIC.

BY THE REV. ARTHUR JOHN LOCKHART.

*From "Progress," 30th October, 1897.*

It is a pity the editorship of so superb an edition of Burns as that of the "Centenary," lately issued at Edinburgh, should have fallen into hands so incompetent as those of Mr. W. E. Henley. It might be supposed the accumulated evidence furnished by the poet and his biographers would have had some weight with Mr. Henley, and that we should have had from his hand a tolerably correct and recognizable literary portraiture of the poet; but alas! fair-minded readers will be much deceived in this matter, and many, I doubt not, will give voice to their disappointment. Mr. Henley, following the fashion of the day, seems determined to take bran new views, and to raise issues that ought to have been considered settled long ago. Mr. Henley has an Essay on the Life, Genius, and Character of the Poet, in which he declares that "The Cottar's Saturday Night" would have sunk into oblivion had not the volume in which it was published contained such poetry as may be found in "Hallowe'en," "Holy Willie," and "The Farmer to his Auld Mare." What a funny old world this is, that, after a century or so, knows not what it ought to admire, till told by Mr. Henley! He declares Burns was purely a vernacular poet—whatever that is —and that "outside the vernacular a rather unlettered eighteenth century Englishman!" This statement refutes itself, with any attentive and appreciative reader of the poet. Some of the parts of the "Cottar's Saturday Night," and other of his poems, which thrill and charm us most, are precisely those parts in which the Scotch does not predominate. His genius expresses itself well in English; but most powerfully in the mingling of English and dialect, for that was the freedom of his native tongue and manner. To the statement that he was "essentially and unalterably a peasant," we will assent only with such qualification as Mr. Henley does not furnish; and we dissent from the conclusion that he was "absolutely of his station and his time;" "the poor-living, lewd, grimy, free-spoken old Scots peasant-world came to a full, brilliant, even majestic close in his work;" and that "we must accept him frankly and without reserve for a peasant of genius perverted from his peasanthood, thrust into a place for which his peasanthood and his genius alike unfitted him, denied a perfect opportunity, constrained to live his qualities into defects, and, in the long run, beaten by a sterile and unnatural environment." Here we have a spider in a nutshell, surely; but how he got there we are not so cocksure as is this advocate, turned judge, of his position. Well, Mr. Henley, we suppose we shall have to believe it, for did not you say so, who for some inexplicable reason have been chosen to deform the most monumental edition of Burns given to the world in this century. But it is this declaration that amazes us. Burns was "a faun!" Oh, ho! We feel relieved. We thought he was Beelzebub, perhaps! We know, on the testimony of many, that he was rather a loose and careless fellow. A recent writer declares: "For a century past poor Burns may be said to have stood in a white sheet, outside a church door, doing penance for his sins." He has been set, like another Hester Prynne, to wear the "Scarlet Letter" in literature. But the figure is altered—Mr. Henley has arranged the puppet another way. He is posed as a faun. "When Pan, his goat-footed father—Pan, whom he featured so closely," says Mr. Henley, " in his great gift of merriment, his joy of life, his puissant appetite, his innate and never-failing humanity—would whistle on him from the thicket he could not often stop his ears to the call." Is Mr. Henley ever struck with a sense of the ridiculous, that he never saw the

## HENLEY AND BURNS. 51

absurdity of putting a part of the poet's character for the whole. Burns had the passion for nature—in common with Pan, maybe (we don't profess to know much of Pan) but also in common with Milton and Mrs. Browning, who were quite proper persons. A faun, for all we know, may be quite an innocent, if not a very positive or energetic, kind of character. A green wood was his only haunt and place of life, and he had a sort of random music in him, perhaps. But maybe we are not so well acquainted with him as Mr. Henley. Is a faun a Jacobin? Is he Scotch to the backbone? Is he a sort of Tyrteus in martial and patriotic enthusiasm? Can he pray? Does he ever turn his attention to the Christian's God? Can he be seduced to a city or a cottage? Tell us, Mr. Henley.

If this is a correct portrait of Burns, what is to become of Carlyle, and all who ever wrote about Burns? for this reverses all their dicta. We remember a very significant remark of Carlyle in "Heroes and Hero Worship," and just now we are minded to apply to it to Mr. Henley: "The valet does not know a hero when he sees him! Alas, no; it requires a kind of hero to do that." And again, he says, after alluding to Burns's "power of true insight" (a faun sees nothing, perhaps, unless it be his little pleasure of the pipe, of sunlight and green leaves), and his "superiority of vision." Mark this: "The fatal, man, the man, is he not always the unthinking man, the man who cannot think and see; but only grope and hallucinate, and mis-see the nature of the thing he works with? He mis-sees it, mistakes it as we say; takes it for one thing, and it is another thing—and leaves him standing like a futility there." We will only say that, perhaps, there has not in our day been an instance of mis-sight and misrepresentation of a notable character equal to that of Mr. Henley.

# THE LATEST ABOUT BURNS.

*From a Chicago Newspaper.*

Mr. W. E. Henley and Mr T. F. Henderson have at length completed that superb "Centenary Edition" of the poetry of Robert Burns which has been so courageously undertaken by Messrs. T. C. and E. C. Jack, of Edinburgh. To the fourth and concluding volume Mr. Henley contributes an exceedingly full Essay on the Life, Genius, and Character of the Poet. It contains such statements as that "The Cottar's Saturday Night" would have sunk into oblivion if the volume in which it was published had not also given to the world such matter as is to be found in "Hallowe'en," "Holy Willie," and "The Farmer to his Auld Mare;" that Burns was a purely vernacular poet, and "outside the vernacular, a rather unlettered eighteenth century Englishman;" that he was "essentially and unalterably a peasant;" that he was "absolutely of his station and his time; the poor-living, lewd, grimy, free-spoken, ribald old Scots peasant-world came to a full, brilliant, even majestic close in his work;" and that "we must accept him frankly and without reserve for a peasant of genius perverted from his peasanthood, thrust into a place for which his peasanthood and his genius alike unfitted him, denied a perfect opportunity, constrained to live his qualities into defects, and, in the long run, beaten by a sterile and unnatural environment."

There will be "wigs on the green" over this Centenary Essay. When Burns told his wife that the world would think better of him in a hundred years he was not thinking of Mr. Henley. He may reasonably have considered that many of his faults of character would then be forgotten; but here they are set forward with really scrupulous care, in splendid print, on beautiful paper, in a volume which it is a real pleasure to see and to handle. For a century past, poor Burns may be said to have stood in a white sheet, outside a church door, doing penance for his sins. Then Mr. Henley comes along, feels a freakish sort of pity for the melancholy figure, and determines to alter its character. He gives a twist to the features, elongates the ears, and conveys an impression of cloven hoofs. He was a faun, says Mr. Henley. "When Pan, his goat-foot father— Pan, whom he featured so closely in his great gift of merriment, his joy in life, his puissant appetites, his innate and never-failing humanity —would whistle on him from the thicket he could not often stop his ears to the call." This is what, in the long run, has come of that strait-laced and Puritanical criticism which has had almost the sole handling of Burns for so many years. There comes a robustuous critic who is not at all Puritanical. He determines to exhibit the poet as he really was, or as, after a long and close study, he honestly conceives him to have been. And we have to admit that the picture is not greatly changed; it is merely the handling that is different. It is no piece of artistic whitewashing, this Essay on the Life, Genius, and Achievements of one of the greatest of national poets. Mr. Henley required no such advice as that which Cromwell tendered to the painter of his portrait. The wart was certainly not to be left out in this case. On the contrary, it was to be painted in with the utmost care and the most cunscientious detail.

Mr. Henley appears to have been spoiling for a fight; but he must not be regarded as one who is deficient in artistic sympathy with Burns. He is a poet himself, and can recognise a great poet when he sees him. Much of the work he has done in this edition is work of the greatest value. He has not deliberately set himself to the belittlement of his subject; but to the correction of what he believes to be the various sorts of wrong impressions. He determines to show exactly what Burns's life was;

what were his limitations; how far he was indebted to his predecessors; what is the exact nature of the debt which the world owes to his genius. The argument throughout has every appearance of being convincing, of not admitting of any reply; and yet it does not convince. We think of a few of Burns's lyrics, and away goes Mr. Henley's theory of an inspired faun, of a son of the goat-footed Pan. For the reason, first of all, that a faun is not human, and Burns is human all over and all through. That is why he is being so much discussed to-day, a century after his death. It is in his humanness that we find the explanation of his universal appeal, to the literate and to the illiterate, to the high and the low, to the Ayrshire peasantry and those wealthy persons who will purchase the four handsome volumes in which Mr. Henley sets forth this outspoken expression of his views.

It may be asked why, in the case of this great poet in particular, we are eternally discussing questions of character. We do not take up "Paradise Lost" in order to remind ourselves of Milton's marital relations. There has been infinite "chatter about Harriet," but it has not obscured Shelley. When Mr. Henley brings out his edition of Byron, will the amours of that poet be dealt with in proportion to those of Burns? A calculation of the number of volumes that would be required may prevent such a catastrophe. The fact is that we so constantly discuss the moral character of this Ayrshire peasant, this inspired faun, because he was himself more than candid on the subject. We know from himself the worst that can be said about him. So far from concealing his faults, he exaggerated them, which was in itself a fault. He freely " gave himself away " in his letters to his friends. But was he really worse than his time? Was he worse, even, than many of those neighbours who prattled to the early biographers about the sinfulness of his life? Was he, as Mr. Henley seems to maintain, worse than he might have been because he was a peasant? If the peasantry of Scotland was "lewd" in the latter half of the last century, which section of Scottish society was less so? But there might be no end to these questions. Certainly, Mr. Henley and his colleague have provided us with all the materials necessary, or available, for forming our own judgment of Burns. If it were possible to say in this case, " his worst he kept, his best he gave," we should still have to admit that his latest editors have kept nothing back. And probably all genuine lovers of Burns will prefer to form their own conception of his character, even though they may not be able to "pruv it" after the skilful and forcible fashion of Mr. Henley.

SPEECH BY MR. F. FAITHFULL BEGG, M.P., TO THE ROSEBERY BURNS CLUB, GLASGOW,

25TH JANUARY, 1898.

In rising to propose for your acceptance the toast of "Caledonia and Caledonia's Bard," a toast famous ever since it was drunk at the historic meeting of the St. Andrew's Lodge in Edinburgh, and received with "multiplied honours and repeated acclamations," I am conscious of sensations similar to those which must be experienced by, for example, a young minister when privileged to preach before the Presbytery, or of those which are probably felt by an older practitioner when called upon to exhort the Fathers of the Church collected together in General Assembly.

Doubtless there are those who rejoice in such an opportunity and would deliver themselves of their message, if message they had, without hesitancy or fear. But I am given by temperament to a more serious mood, and have learned by previous experience to respect both my subject and my audience more highly than any such attitude involves.

Abandoning, however, anything further in the nature of preface, let me address myself immediately to the subject-matter of the toast. Here at once I find prepared for me by those responsible for the arrangement of the proceedings a sweet embarrassment. For I am asked to discuss within the limits of a single after-dinner speech not only one but two subjects of surpassing interest. This conjunction of inspiring themes demands an effort in compression, an experiment in oratorical hydraulics, from which the boldest might well shrink.

I propose, however, to avoid that difficulty by taking a liberty for which I hope you will grant your approval. The natural method suggested by the title of the toast would be to separate the subject into the divisions into which it more obviously falls, and to invite you first to ascend with me to the high tableland of national sentiment, where most fitly might be discussed our native Caledonia, and thereafter, if I may pursue the metaphor, to lead you, with what skill I might, down through the pleasant valley of reminiscence of Caledonia's Bard.

Such an arrangement of the subject, however, must, I fear, have resulted more or less in a repetition of much that has often been better said, whilst fortunately I have been provided by the kindness of the latest of the poet's critics with metal more attractive.

In short, I propose to devote myself to the task of crossing swords with a certain literary freebooter whose inroads upon tradition, and contempt for all moods of criticism, except those of the pitiless iconoclast, cannot, notwithstanding the hall-mark of approval accorded by some, but have stirred to the depths the hearts of all lovers of the poet who have studied his attacks.

It is not, I assure you, without trepidation that I venture into this controversy. The Philistine in the field of literature has all the advantage which the destructive method confers. The finer the material, the more exquisite the carved work, the less easily may it resist the axe of the destroyer.

This particular Philistine, moreover, has the skill of his weapons in no ordinary degree. In attempting to play the part of David, I do not intend to be too particular as to whether the stones from the brook of which I shall make use are of the smoothest.

Doubtless you will have already perceived that it is of Henley, the chief editor of the Centenary Burns, and of his method that I propose to speak, and my general criticism is that it is difficult to decide which stands most condemned, the self-sufficiency of the critic himself, or the unfairness of his method of attack.

Throughout the criticism there runs the tone of the superior person. He treats with unconcealed contempt what he calls the "common Burnsite." He speaks of the carelessness or romantic humour of such editors as Allan Cunningham, Hogg, and Motherwell, and Robert Chambers. Of Scott Douglass he has nothing better to say than that had he known something of literature he might have gone far to establish a sound tradition in the matter of text; whilst all the biographers previous to himself he describes as "the battered jog-trot authorities of the prime."

For my own part, let me say in passing that I do not hesitate to proclaim myself a "Burnsite," enthusiastic, and therefore, according to Henley, probably "common." Common, indeed, in the sense that I share the sentiments of tens of thousands of my countrymen all the world over, and enthusiastic all the more because of this very onslaught itself.

Whilst appreciative and occasionally even cordial in his praise of the genius and achievement of the poet, Henley is perpetually turning aside to gird at Burns himself, his friends, his times, and his style.

The Edinburgh of the period he calls "a city of harlotry, high jinks, and, above all, drink "— " gay, squalid, drunken, dirty, lettered and venerable," whilst the poet's surroundings are described as "the poor-living, lewd, grimy, free-spoken, ribald, old Scots peasant world."

Of such pieces as "Holy Willie's Prayer," "The Holy Fair," and "Tam o' Shanter," he declares that they are the "Kail and Potatoes" of local scandal. Of "Ye Banks and Braes" he says that it is the third set of "Sweet are the Banks," which is true, but goes on to add that "being the worst it is naturally the most popular," which is gratuitously false.

Violent personal attacks upon the poet and savage criticism of his writings alternate with studied regularity. But it is for the poet himself that the choicest vials of abuse are reserved. It is demanded of us that we should abate what he calls the old fantastic estimate of originality. He calls Burns a "hobnailed Gray," who was imitative in kind and traditional in practice. His peasant origin is sneered at with wearying persistence. Burns according to Henley is the "irresponsible Faunus of Mossgiel," whose chief gift was the trick of throwing the lyric handkerchief, and who degenerated into a sentimental sultan expelling beauty after beauty from his lyric harem as with a fork. When Pan, we are told, his goat-foot father, would whistle on him from the thicket he could not often stop his ears to the call, and so on until the reader, wearied and disgusted, longs to lay down the volume and turn to the poet himself for a breath of something fresh and invigorating.

As an illustration of Henley's method I do not think I can do better than refer to his remarks upon the "pleasant pasquil," as he calls it, which is inserted in the notes to Vol. ii. This piece, he tells us, came into the hands of the editors too late for insertion in the Miscellanies, but, he goes on to say, "we have pleasure in giving it in this note." The cause of this pleasure is only too apparent because our critic finds here a cherished opportunity of defaming and belittling the poet. Of the lampoon itself the less said the better. Modelled after the manner of the old English ballad, in the style of "Sir Cauline" or of "The Patient Countess," the poem is a bitter attack upon one Mrs. Grizzel Young. It consists chiefly of a rhyming account of a passage at arms between that lady—who is introduced as "Grim Grizzel" and designated "Lady Glaur-hole," and John o' Clods," her serving-man. The subject-matter of the poem cannot be referred to in polite society, and certainly it was never intended by Burns for publication. The manner of it is described by the critic as "plainly Burns," and "by no means at his worst." Now Henley has persistently declared that, except in the vernacular, Burns was a failure. To much of his work conveyed through that medium it is only fair to admit that unqualified praise is accorded.

But even when writing in the vernacular we are told that his style was borrowed "from stall-artists and neighbour-cuckoos," whatever that may mean. When, however, Burns wanted to be not so much sincere as impressive, we are told that he wrote English. As illustrations Henley cites "Scots Wha Ha'e," in which poem he says Burns, like Jourdain, "talked prose without knowing it," and "The Cottar's Saturday Night," in which he asserts Burns was neither an artist nor a poet. Elsewhere we have the following general criticism, "He might have lived and died an English-writing Scot, and nobody been a thrill or a memory the better for his work." Nobody a thrill or a memory the better for "Scots Wha Ha'e!" Nobody a thrill or a memory the better for "The Cottar's Saturday Night!" Was there ever more monstrous perversity or criticism? But my business at the present moment is with the pasquil. This fugitive poem is, with positively diabolical ingenuity, selected at the last moment and dragged by the heels into the notes, being too late for the text. Written in English, it is suspect, according to the critic's own declaration; being exceptionally coarse in its subject-matter, it is calculated to create prejudice in the mind of the average reader; and of this casual effort we are told that it is veritable Burns and by no means at his worst.

The truth is, that Henley fails as a critic of Burns for two reasons:

*Firstly*, He is not a Scotsman, and has proved himself too much of an alien to adjust his mental focus to Scottish environment;

*Secondly*, He addresses himself to the task of criticism from a wrong standpoint.

I shall endeavour to illustrate both propositions, but first let me offer a word of praise regarding the book itself, which I may say at once is perfect as far as paper and print can make it. As a treasury of research, moreover, the Centenary Burns is invaluable to the student. How far Henley himself may claim the credit for this I cannot say, but I suspect that as regards this portion of the work his fellow-editor, Henderson, has taken the labouring oar. Not that the diligent may not discover oversights and the evidence of hasty and unwarrantable conclusions. The ascription, for example, of the chorus of "Again Rejoicing Nature Sees" to Burns himself, instead of to a friend in Edinburgh, which latter we know to be accurate from the poet's own statement, is a case in point; whilst authorities are not unfrequently incorrectly quoted. In any case endless pains and wide literary knowledge have gone to make clear much that was obscure, and to correct errors of inference or of fact in earlier compilations. As a supreme literary effort, moreover, too much praise cannot be accorded to it. It is when we come to the estimate of the poet's character, of his work, and of his times, that the failure becomes so patent as to be painful; and here it is, as I take it, that the Henley influence dominates the whole. The biographical notice in Vol. iv. is characterised by a virulence of criticism, derogatory of Scotsmen and of Scottish life and manners, which no true Scot can ever forgive. Scotland was a place, we are told, out of which the Whigs had crushed the taste for everything but fornication and theology.

I shall not follow the critic into any question of the nature of Whigs. That would be entirely foreign to my purpose to-night and the nature of this gathering. Burns himself had a good fling at them in "Awa, Whigs, Awa," and perhaps the politics of the period are now so much a matter of history that we should all agree that Whigs, equally with Tories, did harm as well as good. But what possible justification can there be for such a vulgar generalisation as that which I have just quoted? The morals of the time may have been bad, as the poet's life itself unfortunately bears testimony. But were they worse than our own? I doubt it, but will not pursue the inquiry. As for Scottish theology, although Calvinism may be, and apparently is, a sealed book to Henley, Calvinism, however much it may have erred on the side of doctrinal subtlety, has had more to do with the making of great men—with the single exception, perhaps, of oatmeal—than, evidently, Henley wots of. But I have not done with this marvellous definition! If Whiggery was in the ascendant, at least the Jacobite tradition, with its picturesque loyalty to a race which had forfeited by its own incapacity all title to respect, survived as an admirable counterpoise. Literature, as evidenced by the society of the capital, quick to appreciate the genius of the poet and soon to be illuminated by the witchery of the great magician, Sir Walter Scott, was flourishing; whilst such commerce as was possible in a poor country, as yet with its mineral wealth unsuspected, was active. But more than all this, and to the credit of the Scottish nation in an eminent degree, the education of youth was being fostered and developed to an extent unknown in any other country in the world. Whilst in England education was neglected, Scottish youth in all ranks of life enjoyed the advantage of a system which was itself, in the form of the Parish Schools, the direct outcome of that very Calvinism at which our critic's cheap sneers are directed. Lastly, the *perfervidum ingenium* was not dead or even sleeping, for, was not Scotland at the very period in question pouring out an ever-flowing stream of the best of her sons, warriors, statesmen, scientists, men of letters and, above all, colonists, whose influence was not only felt at the time, but has continued to impress itself upon history and civilisation even to the present hour. Yet this is the country out of which we are told had disappeared the taste for everything except fornication and theology.

Nothing can be easier than to condemn a man's writings if you first of all adopt a standard of criticism of your own making: selected with as little relation as possible to the medium in which he has worked. You have then only to show how far he has diverged from your own arbitrary datum line and the thing is done. Such has been the method of our critic. No one, for example, would expect to find Miltonic blank verse in Burns's poems. Neither by education nor by temperament was Burns fitted for such an exercise. Yet the absence of this is emphasised as a reproach. Burns was essentially a poet of nature, free and spontaneous. His motto, chosen by himself with rare appropriateness, was "Wood-notes wild." Milton set himself the task of embodying vast conceptions evolved with infinite labour from a gigantic and often lurid imagination. A comparison of the two is as reasonable as if one should compare the profound speculations of the Book of Job with the rippling lyrics of the Sweet Singer of Israel. What is there in common between the twenty-third Psalm and the philosophy of Eliphaz the Temanite?

Henley himself is a poet and of no mean order.

But his poetry is of camps and towns. Rhythm it may have, but of rhyme it has little. His "Song of the Sword," for example, is full of virility. But nature, in the sense in which Burns understood it, is to him a sealed book. We can well understand that for such a man Burns, with his woods and his streams, has little attraction. A great poet, speaking of Chaucer, has said:

> · · · "And as I read
> I hear the crowing cock, I hear the note
> Of lark and linnet, and from every page
> Rise odours of ploughed field and flowery mead."

One of the greatest merits of Burns's poetry to my mind is that he is for ever drawing you aside to the wood or to the stream, and saying, "It is good for us to be here." But all this has no charm for our critic. For the "common Burnsite" who admires such he has no better adjectives than sentimental, ignorant, uncritical or pig-headed. From Henley's "London Voluntaries" it would appear that Piccadilly at midnight is for him the highest exemplar of the picturesque, and, I presume, the mænads who frequent it more to be desired than, say, Mary Campbell, whom he calls a "bare-legged Beatrice," and describes as an average Scots peasant to whom "a merry-begot was, if not a necessary to life, at all events the commonest effect of ill-luck."

I fear that I may have wearied you. I can

only say that I have by no means exhausted the subject.

There remains, however, one general note running through the whole of the volumes with which I desire to deal. This note has been already indicated in the references to the charges of parochialism and want of originality. These two charges are insisted upon throughout. Whilst admitting that the Kilmarnock poems contain masterpiece after masterpiece, Henley cannot resist turning aside, in the form of a footnote, to emphasise his opinion that "the most are local—parochial even." Apply the test, he says, to almost any of the poems, the masterpieces not excepted, and the result is the same. Now I suppose that being only a "common Burnsite" it is to be expected that I should take the wrong view. But my deliberate opinion is that here is the chief merit of this phase of Burns's work. The reading of these poems is a peculiar pleasure, says Henley, for the student of style, and if that student, he adds, have the faculty of laughter, then he may also enjoy the poet's master quality, which is humour! But for beauty, we are told, we must go elsewhere, we must go to Milton, to Keats, and to Herrick. Now we are not necessarily talking of beauty. Beauty there is in plenty, if Henley could only see it, and beauty is doubtless an excellent thing in poets. But the claim of these poems to our admiration does not necessarily rest in their beauty. It rests in their force of diction, their incisive grasp and mastery of effect, their faithful portraiture of men, manners, and times, their fidelity to nature, their scorn of shams and scathing denunciations of hypocrisy and cant, in most of which qualities I can only name a single poet—Walt Whitman—who approaches Burns in intensity of effect. But in Whitman the quality of humour is almost wholly absent.

There remains the charge of want of originality. This is based upon the admitted fact that much that has come down to us consists of adaptations of the earlier work of others, and relates, of course, chiefly to the contributions to the Museum and the Scottish Airs; contributions which were entirely a labour of love, as Henley freely admits. There was no pretence upon Burns's part that these were wholly original; on the contrary, he himself put it upon record that he had "begged, borrowed, and stolen" all the old songs he could in order to improve and, if possible, perfect them. This fact is made the basis of the assertion that in "tone, sentiment, method, diction, and phrase," Burns borrows from the vernacular school and runs into debt to it for suggestions as to ideas and style, and, generally, that he was a "final expression," not the founder of a dynasty, like Keats, Byron, and Shelley. I do not stop to inquire what these dynasties are or who their reigning sovereigns may be to-day. Each of the poets named was no doubt in himself a vital force. But as compared with Burns, regarded as a creative artist, I make bold to assert that each and all of them, and their heirs of line, if they have any, are as kinglets to an emperor. Burns may prove to have been a "final expression." Certain it is that he summed up and embodied in himself the very best of all that had preceded him. *Nihil tetiget quod non ornavit.* He could take the dry bones of an old song or lyric fragment, and forthwith bone joined to bone and flesh and skin covered them at his magic touch. Dozens of rhymesters had tinkered with the refrain of "Auld Lang Syne" without making it live. Burns recast it into a form in which it has become and remains the ultimate symbol and most perfect expression of human brotherhood throughout, ay and beyond, the English-speaking races of the world. He did the same with "My love is like a red, red rose," to name no others. He gave, in short, perfect lyric form to numberless poetic fragments which had all but disappeared in the dust-heaps of half-forgotten predecessors. If no one has come after him fit to be named as his peer, it is because he shines with a brilliancy which eclipses all rivalry—a star of the first magnitude—as though one should compare Sirius to an unit in the Milky Way. For a hundred years his fame has been ever increasing. At no time has he been more widely known than he is at the present moment. Never has any poet commanded the love and affection of his fellow-countrymen in like degree. Wherever the English language is spoken, there he is cherished and beloved. Year after year his note grows stronger, year after year his admirers become more numerous. His shortcomings and his faults are forgiven and forgotten. Already his genius has triumphed over every obstacle, and, as the years roll on, whilst poetic dynasties will fade and their founders be forgotten, whilst the gibe of the critic and the sneer of the Philistine will sink into oblivion, his influence will remain indelibly engraved upon the literature of his country, and his memory will flourish green in the heart of his myriad admirers.

## MR. R. WALLACE, M.P., ON BURNS'S CRITICS—AN ADDRESS DELIVERED BEFORE THE LEEDS CALEDONIAN SOCIETY,

### January 25th, 1899.

Mr. Wallace, who was cordially received, gave the toast of the evening, "The Immortal Memory of Burns." It was, he said, with a real sense of his responsibility that he proposed that toast to the memory of the greatest poet —and one of the greatest men—which their Scotch nationality had contributed to the immortals. All over the world on that day Scotsmen were engaged in celebrating the anniversary of the birth of Robert Burns, and the enthusiasm of that demonstration did not seem to be languishing or diminishing either in universality or power with the flight of time.

But there were people among other nationalities, and some even among themselves, who rather reflected upon them, hinting, in fact, that they were somewhat overdoing it. Other races, it was said, did not act as the Scotch did, and yet they had poets as illustrious and as influential as Burns. There was one point of difference, however, and it was this—that at the time when Burns appeared there was a far larger proportion of popular receptivity for such poetry as Burns created—the masses of the Scotch people were at that time able at least to read, and many of them to do much more, and that was then a rare thing in the world. They were brought under the influence of a school and Church system, which stimulated in a peculiar degree a certain kind of philosophy, a narrow, intellectual development. They were also the inheritors of a great tradition of song and minstrelsy, and Burns spoke to them in their own language of things with which they were familiar, with a power and a charm that were irresistible. When people asked, therefore, why the Scotch continued to be singular among the peoples in these days by holding these demonstrations, the Scotch might very well ask in return, "What people possesses equally great traditions, and (to quote the language of the Prayer Book) equally 'understanded of the people.'" If other nations were in the same position as Scotland in such a matter, they would be doing the same thing. Burns clubs or their analogues were an inevitable outcome of that position, and it was desirable that they should flourish.

He was profoundly grateful for what Burns was and for what he did. Burns did not, like many other poets, set to work to propound in rhymed or blank verse a vast and vague philosophy, which often yielded to the student of it nothing of any value for his pains. Burns dealt with the feelings and things which met man under every circumstance, real and simple entities—men and women—perhaps not always real and simple from the moral or any other point of view, but still men and women. The "Jolly Beggars," "Black Russels," "Souter Johnnies"—and other Johnnies—Gavin Hamiltons, Dr. Hornbooks, Marys, and Clarindas, and Hannahs innumerable—dogs, young or old, two or more or less—wounded hares, mountain daisies, field mice, and haggis—Scotch religion and toothache, ordinations and holy fairs—he treated of all these and, in short, of an innumerable variety of topics, and drawing from them the most pointed, amusing, instructive or effective reflections. Burns always used the right word in the right way, putting the thing instantly and almost visibly before them, and to those who thought that this kind of thing—the simplicity of fire-side talk—was very easy, he would say, "Just you try."

He liked Burns's brevity. There were poets who were too amazingly long for "human nature's daily food." Homer and Milton were, no doubt, great, but they were no joke, and it was rather slow to take to their sweets after the "Jolly Beggars" or the "Twa Dogs," which were glorified tit-bits, poetic tabloids, containing the essence of observation and feeling. Burns's lambent humour gleamed on every page, and in proof of this Mr. Wallace recited passages from the "Address to Scotch drink" and the "Address to the Deil." Somebody had said that if they wanted beauty they must go elsewhere than to Burns for it. Burns had an eye for the beauty of Nature, but he was more concerned with man, the chief work of Nature, and man was not always, either physically or morally, a beauty. Homer would have said, "Set on the wine," where Keats said—

> "Oh, for a beaker full of the warm south,
> Full of the true, the blushful Hippocrene,
> With beaded bubbles winking at the brim,
> And purple-stained mouth"—

which would have rather puzzled the waiter. Why were our clothes to-day better than those of the days of Elizabeth? Simply because whatever advantage we had to-day was due to our own selves, and not to the decoration. Burns had not gew-gaw beauty, but he had the genuine beauty of "Highland Mary," "Ye banks and braes," and of that immortal quatrain which Byron declared to be the finest thing of the kind in human speech—"Had we never loved sae kindly."

Mr. Wallace then read a considerable portion of an article which Mr. Henley contributed to a weekly paper about a year ago on the subject of Burns dinners, in which the leading spirits on such occasions were described as including half-read M.P.'s and similarly qualified divines, who drank the immortal memory pottle-deep (and a pottle meant four pints of whisky); and, finally, Mr. Henley described Carlyle as being the father of all them that babble in Burns Clubs. The name applied to members of such Societies was that of the "Common Burnsite." As Burns himself said, he would say to Mr. Henley, "Ye may be wrang," and, personally, he would rather be wrong with Carlyle than right with Henley. Mr. Henley was always saying that Burns was misplaced in being born a peasant. No doubt if Mr. Henley had had the arrangement of the world he would have had Burns born in London about the middle of the present century, in time to become a subordinate co-operator with Henley in bringing out a work to show up Shakespeare. At anyrate, he could say he was innocent of the charge of calling Burns "Robbie," though some of them might do it in the excess of their affection. What they said was that Burns was theirs and theirs only, and they didn't care whether he was the "greatest poet in time" or not. He was what nobody, and no other poet, could be to them, and that had nothing to do with outside impertinent intruders. Of course, Burns had had predecessors. Without Homer there might have been no Virgil or Dante, Milton or Shakespeare. And it had never entered into any Burnsite's head to think that Burns stood an unaided miracle, deriving no assistance from any quarter whatever. Burns himself had spoken of Theocritus and Virgil and Shenstone, of Ramsay and Fergusson, though he had done no more than kindle at their flame.

As to the character of Burns, they did not try to put him up as a man possessed of those middle-class virtues which Mr. Henley considered such contemptible things. Mr. Henley more than insinuated that Burns was a self-ruined blackguard, and that they should put that before them on occasions of that kind. But if that were so, a good many of them would not be there that night. Mr Henley was rather hard on the Inland Revenue officers. He (Mr. Wallace) didn't see why an exciseman should not be a saint—if he liked. St. Matthew, he understood, was a very presentable saint, though he had sat at the receipt of custom—and Burns was something larger and more useful to the world, and therefore better than most of the Saints in the calendar. Mr. Wallace warmly denounced Mr. Henley's observations on the character of the peasant morality in Scotland. As the minister who had preached the funeral sermon of Mrs. Begg in Alloway Kirk, and as one who had known Mrs. Begg for years, he took that opportunity of flinging back his foul slander in Mr. Henley's face. As to Burns's character, they might take Burns's account of it. Where was the man who could say to him "I am holier than thou?" He made no defence for Burns, because he had met no man who could attack him. But he denied that Burns died a ruined man, as was said by most of his critics. Though he died poor he did not die insolvent, and the world took charge of the treasure which he left behind him. It would be a pity if they were ever to forget so memorable a life-work and so memorable a man. His career was conceived in a lofty spirit, which ran towards splendid issues. At noon his sun went down while he was still fighting a brave battle with fortune and for the realising of his own ideal of life, leaving behind him a record of brilliant achievements, noble lineaments of character, and a not unconsoling calculation as to what he might further have done had fate permitted him to fulfil his day and generation. They cherished the splendid fragment he left behind all the more carefully and affectionately because its scantiness made it more precious, and thus in the solemn silence in which it was customary to recall the memory of the great departed, he asked them to fulfil their part that night in perpetuating the unforgettable by once more drinking the "immortal memory of Burns."

## SHERIFF BRAND ON THE SUBJECT.

Sheriff Brand, in proposing "The Immortal Memory of Burns" before the Ayr Burns Club, January 25, 1898, said that to very few was it given to shine with such lustre as to ensure fame to a distant future. During the last hundred years and more, our natural instincts have in the case of Burns unerringly discriminated between accident and essence, between the environment of Burns the ploughman and the immortal brilliance and purity of Burns the singer. While not forgetting or ignoring the former, we and our fathers have wisely allowed many details to slip into a subordinate place, as being only of secondary significance. These instincts John Gibson Lockhart undoubtedly confirmed and strengthened by his Life of Burns published in 1828, and Carlyle by his memorable review of that volume in the same year. Like a loyal student of nature and of man as he was, the hermit of Chelsea had only made use of the surroundings of Burns in order the more strikingly to pourtray and illustrate the glory and endurance of the work he achieved. So likewise did he point out how Burns made our

Scottish literature to grow "with the true racy virtues of the soil and climate." From a viewpoint not dissimilar were written the biographies or criticisms of Currie, of Walker, of Allan Cunningham, and later of Chambers, Scott-Douglas, Nichol, and Wallace. Taken together, they led to the verdict that it is not the shortcomings of Burns that permeate our memory and imagination, but the proud courage, the splendid manhood, the inimitable and unsurpassable humour, the instinctive flash, the sympathy that knows no antipathy, not even to the louse, or the criminal (as in "Macpherson's Farewell"), or the very Devil himself. Sheriff Brand continued—Our Burns is the lyric spirit purged from the dross of earth and time, sublimated as by a heavenly alchemy, and affectionately woven into the substance of our hearts. No possibility can there be of our losing this treasure, so long as we do not lose ourselves. But even if such possibility existed, the literary efforts of the past year have taken the utmost pains to remove it. In the Centenary Edition, by William Henley and Thomas Henderson, we have the latest sustained effort to set forth the poet's life and writings and character in all their fulness. Such an effort, if well directed, and based on a brotherly and true estimate of the poet's character and influence, should have our cordial recognition. But does Mr. Henley reach this level? He and his fellow-scribe say in their preface that "for the exact and adequate understanding of the bard we thought it right to give the history, so far as known, and the local setting of his several pieces, together with an explanation of his chief allusions—many of them of the most fleeting kind." From this we are to understand that till these men rose from the dust no one had been found capable of duly introducing the poet to an ignorant world, not any of those above mentioned, nor even the supreme critics, Scott or Jeffrey, or Wordsworth, or Campbell, or Wilson. This, you will agree, is pretty good for a beginning. But who are Mr. Henley and Mr. Henderson? The former is described as " the *beau sabreur* of the weekly press." The latter, apparently, has not found any one to boom his priceless qualities. The edition concludes its fourth and last volume with an Essay on Burns by Mr. Henley, and to that Essay I would very briefly invite your attention. That Mr. Henley has studied Burns I do not deny. He has not only read and considered everything available that Burns wrote in poems, in songs, in verses, and in epigrams, but he has bestowed minute attention on Burns's numberless letters written as private communications, and never intended to see the light. After quoting some of Mr. Henley's observations, Sheriff Brand said—The sinister purpose of this literary dabbler has not been to master in all their fulness the life, character, and works of Burns, to weigh these in the scales of impartial criticism, and to assign Burns his true position in the history of our country's poetic literature, in the development of the eighteenth century, and in his influence on the national mind. His purpose has been to sneer down Burns to a level infinitely below that which he has always held, not only in the heart of Scotland, but in the human heart all the world over. While admitting, as he cannot but admit, that Burns's poems and songs illuminate his memory with a deathless fame, he grudges this fame to Scotland and Scotsmen, and endeavours to tarnish its brightness by bringing into close perspective with it everything that can be culled from heedless verses, from a rollicking life, and from private letters, of a nature calculated, if possible, to make the reader, or the student, think less of the songs the more he knows of the singer. In conclusion, he said, Mr. Henley forgets that Burns, though he came in the lowly garb of struggling poverty, breathed a new and more vivid life into our national existence, and intensified a spirit of patriotism which has never since ceased to glow. He forgets that no other mortal has so profoundly and enduringly swayed and influenced the minds of all. The green-eyed critic may if he please call him "a local poet," but his locality is the universal heart of the Anglo-Saxon race. If this essayist thought to attract notice to himself by forsaking for a time the anonymous columns of the weekly press, and writing on the life of Burns, I cannot say he has not succeeded; but that success must be ephemeral, for his judgment is at fault and his criticisms are false. We Scots formed our estimate of the poet long before Mr. Henley arose to enlighten us, and that estimate will remain long after the critic and his efforts have passed into oblivion and added one shred more to the rag heap of the past. Some of our mighty dead are more alive now than even when in full strength they strode this palpitating earth, and of these Burns is the foremost.

## THE REV. J. H. M'CULLOCH'S PROTEST —FROM AN ADDRESS DELIVERED BEFORE THE LEITH BURNS CLUB,

### JANUARY 25TH, 1898.

The rev. gentleman, in proposing "The Immortal Memory of Robert Burns," said Burns had a heart that beat in sympathy with, and which could interpret, the hearts of his fellows. They felt that there was a living man behind all, and that he wrote for men and women of like passions as himself. That was the root idea underlying the desire which so many admirers of the poet felt to have a statue—a visible presentment of him in their midst—a desire to which they hoped ere long to give expression in Leith. Unfortunately the times in which Burns lived were times when to be social meant to be convivial to a large extent as well. "Scotch drink" made its appearance on every occasion, and it was freely partaken of by all classes. It was because of this that many of his social poems were Bacchanalian in their character. Not that Burns himself could fairly be represented as an inveterate toper. The greatest misfortune which could befall the memory of Burns would be that he should be remembered principally for his Bacchanalian poems. It was to be feared that there was a time when in celebrations like the present those were largely thought of, and men believed that they did honour to the memory of the bard when, like Tam o' Shanter, they got "fou and unco happy." Such a way of thinking about him was now happily becoming a thing of the past among the true admirers of his transcendent genius. It was not good for them that "men's evil manners should live in brass." The less they thought of them the better, for then the virtues that made them great shone out more distinctly. It would be fatal to the immortal memory of their poet if for many it became a thing of taverns and whisky. He had said that stricter investigation had led to a higher estimate of the personal life of Burns than was at one time entertained. But he must modify that statement. During the year a Centenary Edition of Burns had been published, which contained an Essay on "His Life, Genius, and Achievement," by Mr. W. E. Henley, which still more recently had been issued in paper covers. That Essay was of the most extraordinary character, and might be accounted for to some extent by the fact that it was the work of an Englishman. Byron once wrote a scathing satire bearing the title, "English Bards and Scotch Reviewers;" here they had a

Scottish bard and an English reviewer, and one would fancy that Scotland must have done that reviewer some mortal injury when he assailed the Burns cult with such iconoclastic fury. From beginning to end it was a smart attempt of "the new journalist" to make out that Burns was a man steeped in vice and increasingly given over to drink; a man in whom "the bad was bad enough to wreck the good;" "a lewd, amazing peasant of genius, an inspired faun;" who became "a kind of sentimental Sultan;" the crowning specimen of "the poor living, lewd, grimy, free-spoken, ribald, old Scots peasant world;" a man "too resolute to make the most of the passing hour to refrain from drink and talk where drink and talk were to be had;" whose "genius was at once imitative and emulous;" whose "Scots Wha Ha'e" was "for all practical purposes the work of an eighteenth century Scotsman writing in English, and now and then propitiating the fury and watchful genius of Caledonia by spelling a word as if it was spelt in the vernacular;" and so on, and so on. After reading that Essay two things excited surprise. First, that it should have appeared in "The Centenary Edition of Burns" as a worthy account of his "life, genius, and achievement." It would have been more appropriate if it had appeared, as it had ultimately done, in the ephemeral shape of "paper covers." And secondly, that any man could have written "a lewd, inspired faun, whose voice had been ringing through the courts of Time these hundred years and more, and was far louder and far clearer now than when it first broke on the ear of man" in one sentence, without really stopping to inquire how such a thing was possible. It was possible to put those two things together in a single sentence; but humanity never made such a mistake. No, Mr. Henley must try again, and this time it would not be amiss if he adopted the opposite rôle and thought of all that could be said for the poet. He might then find, as men generally did, that the truth lay *in medio*. Ere he closed, he must refer to another aspect of the work of Burns—he meant his relation to the religious side of the national life. He believed that by many that had been misunderstood. Burns was not a religious man; but they utterly mistook him if they thought he was in any sense opposed to religion. Religion was with him a temporary emotion; it never became a real spring of action. He wrote much which some had misinterpreted as antagonistic to religion; but was careful to draw a distinction between the real and the hypocritical in the matter of religious profession, and again and again in his writings they found the expression of those deeper feelings of reverence which he had seen exhibited by his own father.

## MR. JOHN SINTON ON THE SUBJECT.

Mr. Sinton replied to the toast of "The Immortal Memory" before the Carlisle Burns Club, January 25th, 1899, and, at the commencement of his speech, criticised the recently published work on Burns by Mr. Henley, who had made the damaging admission that he read the verse of Burns and all Scots verse in a language or dialect not his own. That critic seemed to be altogether devoid of reverence. He described Carlyle's famous essay on Burns as "a peasant's shout over a peasant." The savage virulence of the malignant attack made by Mr. Henley upon the memory of the dead poet is only paralleled by that of the Scribes and Pharisees upon the living Christ. It may be Mr. Henley's misfortune, not his fault, that by birth, training, and profession, he is incompetent to depict the character of "a Scots peasant" whose complex nature is altogether beyond his ken. The unrestrained expression of his English prejudice against Scotland and the Scotch, runs, like the weft of the web, throughout this unique denunciation of the man Burns.

The dictionary definition of the critic's trade is, "to be inclined to find fault, to be captious, to be censorious," and here we have all three in full blast. Superadded, we have the damaging admission that "the Scots dialect, or language," is not the critic's own. The general outcome of all this being that the Burns of Henley is only Henley's Burns!

Burns pitied "the verra Deil" and gave him his choice of titles. Henley gives Burns worse than deil's titles, and allows no choice. Here are a few of Henley's choicest epithets. "An inspired faun," "The local Lothario," "Old Hawk," "A kind of hobnailed Gray," "A kind of Tarbolton Satan," "Pan, his goathead father," "A peasant resolute to be a buck," "A peasant from first to last," "Essentially and unalterably a peasant," "His songs were derived and written by a peasant, devising and writing for peasants." Henley's conception of "a peasant" is an inferior being made of coarser clay, a round-shouldered, hobnailed, English lout descending steadily to the workhouse or the grave. Hence his sneers at the "peasanthood" of Burns are more bitter than they appear to be on the surface. Would Mr. Henley be surprised to hear that Scottish peasants, as a class, have been, for more than three hundred years, and are now superior in knowledge and manliness, in culture and conduct, to nineteen-twentieths of his own countrymen to-day, including all classes, and not even excluding critics. Maybe they have not yet realised that "a man's a man for a' that." But, as a matter of fact, Burns was not a peasant. He was the son of a small farmer, and worked on his father's farm as such—became a farmer himself, and was within sight of a collector's salary of from £500 to £800 a year (present value) in the Excise when he died.

Not content with attempting to besmirch the memory of Burns, this critic goes out of his way to gibe and sneer at the poet's contemporaries and his nation. The Duchess of Gordon becomes "Her frolic Grace of Gordon." The Earl of Buchan is "That curious irascible ass." Highland Mary becomes "Either (1) something of a light o' skirts, or (2) she is a social Scottish Mrs. Harris"—"a gay girl." "She consoled Burns for Jean's desertion." "Burns's habits and the habits of the Scots peasant women." Ah! and that is this man's estimate of the mothers of Burns himself, Thomas Carlyle, Hugh Miller, James Hogg, and the "peasant" women of the people generally. Again, contrast Henley's Scots capital—"gay, squalid, drunken, dirty, lettered, venerable," with the "Edina, Scotia's darling seat, all hail thy palaces and towers," of Burns. The Scotland of Burns's day he describes as a country given over " to fornication and theology." He prates about "the primordial instinct" and everything pertaining to the subject with evident relish, and, curiously enough, he declares—"I, for my part, would not give my *Holy Fair*, still less my *Hallowe'en* or my *Jolly Beggars*—observed, selected, excellently reported, for a wilderness of 'Saturday Nights.'" Every man to his taste. The leading characteristics of this Life of Burns appear to be the self-glorification of the writer and the degradation of the poet. The very extravagance of this Englishman's indecent and bitter language deprives it of all judicial weight. Professor Wilson we know; Thomas Carlyle, Wallace, and Lord Rosebery we know. Henley we now know; and we, "the common Burnsites" of to-day, also know that Henley's little will-o'-the-wisp is nothing more than a flickering delusion destined to oblivion mingled with contempt. Referring briefly to another subject, Mr. Henley says that Burns was "sometimes reprimanded (*et pour cause*)." The hollowness and inaccuracy of this oft-repeated charge has been sufficiently demonstrated. The gravity of this false charge consisted in the support it gave to the down-grade theory of the poet in his later years. Seeing that the poet spent the last six years of his life as an Excise official, his now proved diligence in attending to his harassing and distasteful duties, under constant supervision, coupled with his continued promotion, demonstrate the necessary falsity of many charges that have been levelled against him.

This branch of our subject may well be closed with an extract from the famous letter written by Burns, three years before his death, to Erskine of Mar:—" My honest fame is my dearest concern; and a thousand times have I trembled at the idea of those *degrading* epithets that malice or misrepresentation may affix to my name. I have often, in blasting anticipation, listened to some future hackney scribbler, with the heavy malice of savage stupidity, exulting in his hireling paragraphs. . . . . In your illustrious hands, sir, permit me to lodge my disavowal and defiance of these slanderous falsehoods."

Burns suffered more from remorse and genuine penitence than probably any man who ever lived. Not only so, but the very bitterness of his cry, "God be merciful to me a sinner," had been seized upon by his calumniators, and used as a weapon to stab him behind his back. But leave Burns to his Maker, and keeping in view the parable of the Pharisee and the Publican, it is just possible, nay probable, that those who talk so glibly about the sins of Burns may find, at the great day of reckoning, that the penitent poet and the penitent publican are justified rather than they. There are certain classes of people who must always look upon Burns with doubt and suspicion. Many decent, worthy people, naturally and properly disliking the clay, miss the gold. Many worthy teetotallers dislike the poet on account of his drinking songs; but even they are beginning to forgive him for writing "Willie brewed a peck o' maut," and such like. The Pharisee and the hypocrite, throughout their generations, will always dislike him, not because of his sins, but on account of his satires.

> "Oh ye wha are sae guid yersel,
> Sae pious and sae holy,
> You've nought to do but mark an' tell
> Yer neebour's fauts and folly;
> Whose life is like a weel-gaun mill
> Supplied in store o' water:
> The heapit clappers ebben' still,
> An' still the clap plays clatter."

The "gigman" and the clothes-horse can never take to Burns. He is not sufficiently genteel for silly ladyism and spurious nobility.

> "What though on hamely fare we dine,
> Wear hodden gray, an' a' that,
> Gie fules their silk, an' knaves their wine,
> A man's a man for a' that."

The ultra-Calvinist can never take to Burns, for Burns broke the back of "the auld licht." The genuine Calvinist of the poet's time showed only the dark side of the shield. Burns showed the bright.

> "Where human weakness has come short,
> Or frailty stepp'd aside,
> Do thou, All Good, for such thou art,
> In shades of darkness hide.

> "Where with intention I have err'd,
>   No other plea I have,
> But 'Thou art good, and goodness still
>   Delighteth to forgive.'"

The golden calf is as much worshipped in England to-day as it was in the desert 4000 years ago.

> "If happiness have not her seat
>   And centre in the breast,
> We may be wise and rich and great,
>   But never can be blest."

Burns will never be praised by those who dote upon forms, vestments, and such like priestly trumpery, for he wrote "The Cottar's Saturday Night":—

> "Compared with this, how poor religion's pride
>   In all the pomp of method and of art,
> When men display to congregations wide
>   Religion's every grace except the heart.
> The Power incensed the pageant will desert,
>   The pompous strain, the sacerdotal stole;
> But, haply in some cottage, far apart,
>   Will hear, well pleased, the language of the soul,
> And in his book of life the inmate poor enrol."

A child of the common people himself, Burns never deserted his class. He taught the poor man that

> "The rank is but the guinea stamp,
>   The man's the gowd for a' that."

He ennobled honest labour.

> "The honest man, though e'er sae puir,
>   Is king o' men for a' that."

He was the high priest of humanity.

> "Man's inhumanity to man
> Makes countless thousands mourn."

> "Affliction's sons are brothers in distress;
> A brother to relieve, how exquisite the bliss."

> "It's coming yet for a' that,
> That man to man the warld o'er
> Shall brithers be, an' a' that."

Ay, Burns is like a great mountain, based on earth, towering towards heaven—of a mixed character, containing gold, silver, brass, iron, and clay, and from which every man, according to his taste, can become enriched by the gold and the silver, or get mired in the clay. All that is best in Burns (and that is nearly the whole) will remain a precious possession with the Anglo-Saxon race in the ages yet to come. The stars and stripes of our cousins across the sea, the great American people, will ere long float side by side with the grand old flag that for a thousand years has braved the battle and the breeze. And the Bible and Burns will lie side by side in the homes of the reunited Anglo-Saxon race, the freest, bravest, and most liberty-loving people the world ever saw or shall see.

> "With silence, then, shall this toast be met,
> Of 'The Bard' whose sun shall never set,
> Flashing its glory from shore to shore,
> A joy of the world for evermore.
> With silence! No! or said or sung,
> His name shall be on every tongue,
> And in the hearts of all mankind
> The deathless fame of Burns enshrined."

# CONCERNING THE ESSAY.

### By John S. Macnab, New York.

Mr. W. E. Henley, who is spoken of in London as a master prose writer and as a well-known poet, and by admiring friends as a "princely critic" of modern art and literature, has recently fallen upon the poetry and character of Burns in such a savage and slashing style that every "common Burnsite" who has read it—and there are many, "sentimental, ignorant, uncritical" though they may be—must wonder at the amazing misrepresentation, the mixture of sarcasm, prejudice, and a dash of something very like national spleen, a weakness often exhibited by the average Londoner.

He made an attack in his recent Essay in the Centenary Edition, all in a manner that betrayed a willingness to belittle the memory of the Poet, so manifestly vicious is the wording of it. Of course it is all in the interest of truth, so he says, and quickly quotes "Facts are chiels"; but a good deal of it is more suggestive of adroit workmanship—the display

## HENLEY AND BURNS.

of a certain pride in the brilliant technique of "a princely critic" and his coadjutor.

Conan Doyle has written of Henley's style as being "large, loud and passionate, as running to big thoughts and large metaphors." It is easy to believe some of this after a perusal of his Essay, for he slashes right and left, cutting up as if there was nothing else to do, killing that which he affects to prune, as if saying all the time—"See what a work I do;" what Rudyard Kipling might describe as "too much Ego in his Cosmos."

In fits and starts, he does not fail in his admiration for Burns, although he manages in quite a remarkable way to dissemble his love, calling him "the lewd, amazing peasant of genius, the inspired faun whose voice has gone ringing through the courts of Time these hundred years and more." But all this is certain to stop very soon, for Henley has proved to his own satisfaction that Burns had no originality, and what is worse, had not even good English, and in his large imagination he pictures Burns as reading Milton with a view to getting himself up as a "Tarbolton Satan"! There is much in this style, equally "vigorous and virile," showing that Henley, too, has not been without his "forbears."

Some of his well-known lines come up at present, on the London cat. Can they be emulous of "The Twa Dogs"?

> "And behold
> A rake-hell cat—how furtive and acold!
> A spent witch homing from some hideous dance—
> Obscene, quick-trotting, see her tip and fade
> Through shadowy railings into pit of shade."

After doing this on the poor, harmless cat, it helps us to understand him girding at the Poet, and accusing him of being possessed with "the pride of Lucifer" and other qualities "which even to name wad be unlawfu'."

His picture of Scotland at the time of Burns, and his estimate of "The Cottar's Saturday Night," illustrate the critic chortling in his ignorance, and also the malicious spirit with which he approaches the subject. Old Saunders Tait of Tarbolton is discovered to be a critic after Henley's own heart—a veritable "forbear" of the New Realism in criticism. And also the use that is made of the "pleasant pasquil," which the critic "takes pleasure in giving it in this note," is surely the unkindest cut imaginable, and measures the taste which he exhibits in describing the old Scots peasant-world.

It has been proven over and over again by competent authorities that Burns was neither the author nor editor of "The Merry Muses," and for any one to say so is the grossest misrepresentation and calumny. A great deal of the coarse stuff that has been printed as Burns's is not his in any but a misleading sense. Much of it existed before his day, and he himself thus writes to Thomson in November, 1794: "I myself have lately seen a couple of ballads sung through the streets of Dumfries, with my name at the head of them as author, though it is the first time I had ever seen them." "The satirist and singer of a parish" has been proven to be free of the authorship of the filth that Mr. Henley gloats over as being so clever.

This kind of criticism will never lessen the position of Burns as a great lyric poet. The verdict of the world has already been pronounced, that as a writer of songs his memory will last for all time. He is the greatest lyric poet that Britain has produced. Goethe has said, "He who wishes to understand a poet must first set his foot in his province." After a hundred years and more, is it to be imagined that Mr. Henley is the first to meet this demand?

Burns as a poet, like every great artist, had doubtless his limitations. To produce something original all the time, "there's the rub," which even Shakespeare failed at, for, as there is nothing new under the sun, he could only make use of existing material, fashion, unmake, refashion, idealise. And it is in this domain that the critic has much to say of Burns—"borrowing his style as well as his ideas from stall-artists and neighbour cuckoos;"

that is to say, stepping into the vast storehouse of imagery and song, he became at once a discoverer, architect, and builder. It was here that he manifested the possession of the intellectual second-sight which, more than anything else, makes a man a poet. Compared with all that have gone before or since, he had the clearer, finer poetic vision; and his soul was moved to rhythmic strains by the gentle hints and suggestions that came to him. Almost everything in nature might have become the subject of a poem, the regions of nature and humanity appeared so fertile to the poetic sense of this peasant, granted he lacked the culture which some of the moderns find awanting.

But think of his true power and charm, the three qualities as Whittier describes them: "his sensibility, simplicity, and reality. His joys and tears, his passion and pathos, his love and his pride, the reckless mirth of his jovial hours, and the remorseful sadness of his afterthoughts—all are real."

His poems are ever fresh, like the torrents flashing down the mountain side, or as the lochan whose lovely waters hold the trembling moon, they thrill and soothe us as nothing else can. And hence the "common Burnsite." He must have some ventilation for his enthusiasm —that quality has not begun to die out yet, and in clubs and societies all over the world Scotsmen tell of the debt they owe to Burns, and warm themselves anew at the celestial fires of his genius.

How great a service Burns rendered to his country by purifying and idealising Scottish Song. only those who have studied the old collection which he used can realise; and if, here and there, he has written and left unrevised a coarse verse, when we consider when he lived, we can only wonder that the songs he published are so pure. He was most generous in his acknowledgment of his indebtedness to his predecessors, Ramsay and Fergusson, as all the world knows; but a comparison of their work, especially Ramsay's, shows how great was the advance Burns had made. All honour to the unknown authors of the fine old fragments, but what are they compared with the hundreds of lyric gems, the work of Burns, in which he " flings the windows of his soul wide open to the sun."

## THE PENURIOUS COCKNEY.

Ere disappointment, cauld neglect, and spleen
Had soured my bluid an' jaundiced baith my een,
My saul aspired, upo' the wings o' rhyme,
To mount unscaithed to airy heichts sublime;
An', like the lark, to drap, in music rare,
Braw sangs to cheer folks whan their herts were sair.
I struggled lang, but fand it a' nae use,
Nocht paid, I saw, save arrogant abuse.

"Blind fule," I cried, "to fling your pearls to swine.
Awa' wi' dreams o' laurell'd days divine!
Bid Fame guid-bye, and a' sic feckless trash,—
Henceforth write naething but what brings ye cash."

I glowr'd about for something worth my while—
Some *thing* held dear—on whilk to "spew" my bile,

An' fixt my e'e upo' a certain bard,
Syne bocht a Jamieson,* an' studied hard;
An' wha that hears me the vernacular speak
Wad think I learn'd the hale o't in a week.

Weel up in Scotch, I set mysel' to wark
To strip the *Poet* to his very sark,
An' gie the warld a pictur' o' the *Man*
An' a' his *Doin's*—on the cut-throat plan.
My book, gat up regairdless o' expense,
Was hailed *the* book by ilka man o' sense;
Some "half-read" gowks ayont the Tweed micht sneer,
An' name mysel' in words no' fit to hear;
I only leuch. The man himsel' was deid—
*He* couldna reach me, sae I didna heed.

As farmer bodies spread their fiel's wi' dung,
My savoury mess owre ilka page was flung;
An' soon a crap shot upward to the licht,
O' gowden bitties—braw an' blessed sicht.

To me auld Scotlan's been a godsend, jist—
A meal-pock, bottomless, that wad be miss'd.
I maist forget how mony brown bawbees

* Jamieson's "Scottish Dictionary."

I've had for slatin' Provosts and M.P's.
But I'm no' done wi' a' thae cattle yet;
Some ither day I'll gar them lowp a bit!
A brisker dance the deevils hae before 'em
Than Hielan' Fling or Reel o' Tullochgorum.